TESTING
and
MEASUREMENT

TESTING
and
MEASUREMENT
A User-Friendly Guide

Sharon E. Robinson Kurpius ✳ Mary E. Stafford

Arizona State University

SAGE Publications
Thousand Oaks ■ London ■ New Delhi

For information:

Sage Publications, Inc.
2455 Teller Road
Thousand Oaks, California 91320
E-mail: order@sagepub.com

Sage Publications Ltd.
1 Oliver's Yard
55 City Road
London EC1Y 1SP
United Kingdom

Sage Publications India Pvt. Ltd.
B-42, Panchsheel Enclave
Post Box 4109
New Delhi 110 017 India

Printed in the United States of America.

Library of Congress Cataloging-in-Publication Data

Kurpius, Sharon E. Robinson.
Testing and measurement: A user-friendly guide / Sharon E.
Robinson Kurpius, Mary E. Stafford.
        p. cm.
Includes bibliographical references and index.
ISBN 978-1-4129-1002-6 (pbk.)
   1. Educational tests and measurements—Study and teaching (Higher)
2. Mensuration—Study and teaching (Higher)
I. Stafford, Mary E. II. Title.
LB3051.K87 2006
371.26′071′1—dc22   2005008152

This book is printed on acid-free paper.

        08   09   10   9   8   7   6   5   4   3   2

Acquisitions Editor:	Lisa Cuevas Shaw
Editorial Assistant:	Karen Wong
Production Editor:	Laureen Shea
Copy Editor:	Truman Sands, Print Matters, Inc.
Typesetter:	C&M Digitals (P) Ltd.
Proofreader:	Libby Larson
Indexer:	Nara Wood
Cover Designer:	Janet Foulger

Contents

List of Figures

List of Tables

A Note to Students

Believe it or not, you are about to embark on a wonderful adventure. The world of testing and measurement offers you insight into those numbers and scores and tests that have been part of your life since you were a small child. In this user-friendly guide, we're going to introduce you to the basic concepts of measurement and testing in a way we hope will sometimes make you smile or even laugh. We even made ourselves chuckle as we tried to create examples that you can relate to.

Our goal is to help you understand tests and their scores. A test is a sample of behavior or characteristic at a given point in time. We know your behavior has been sampled many times in many classes and that numbers or scores have been used to describe your knowledge, aptitudes, behaviors, attitudes, and even your personality characteristics. This book will help you make sense of these numbers and scores and what is needed to have a strong, good test.

This workbook style textbook is not the end-all in what there is to know about measurement and testing. Instead, we are trying to give you foundational information that you and your professors can build on. If you read the material carefully, take the time to complete the "Let's Check Your Understanding" quizzes, and work through "Our Model Answers" with us, you should be able to master the content covered.

We have tried to present the material in this text in the most user-friendly way we know. Some of our examples may seem corny, but please indulge us. We wanted to make your learning as enjoyable as possible. The yellow brick road awaits you. Have courage, be smart, and open your heart to learning. We are the good witches and we'll be helping you on your journey.

Acknowledgments

First, we would like to thank the multiple reviewers who gave us invaluable suggestions that helped us clarify our ideas and strengthen our final product. Next, we would like to express our gratitude to Dr. Joanna Gorin for reading many of the chapters and providing us with insightful feedback that we used to rethink how we were presenting some major concepts. Her ideas and expertise in measurement made a significant positive contribution to this final work. Joanna, we truly appreciate the time and energy you took to assist us in this project.

We would like to thank Lisa Cuevas Shaw for seeing and appreciating our approach to teaching testing and measurement concepts. She constantly supported us to be creative and to play with ways of making this information fun and interesting for students. Lisa, thank you for believing in us.

Finally, we want to express our gratitude to Jason Love for lending us his wonderful artistic talent by creating the cartoons for this book and to Karen Wong, Laureen Shea, and the staff at Sage for their wonderful assistance in getting this book published. Thanks to all of you.

Lest we forget, we want to thank the many students who over the years appreciated and learned from our humorous approach to teaching testing and measurement. They reinforced our belief that this material didn't have to be dull or boring.

—*SRK*

—*MES*

The contributions of the following reviewers are gratefully acknowledged:

Jim A. Haugh, Rowan University

Dail Fields, Regent University

Eve M. Brank, University of Florida

Anita Hubley, University of British Columbia

CHAPTER 1

What Is a Number?
Is a Rose Always a Rose?

Remember when you first learned nursery rhymes such as "Three Blind Mice" or watched Count Dracula on *Sesame Street?* As a child, you probably helped the person reading to you count each of the three mice or followed the Count as he numbered everything in sight. You were learning numbers. Do you remember holding up your little fingers when someone asked you how old you were? At a very early age, you were expected to begin to understand numbers and what they meant. Numbers are a part of everyone's life. We all use them without thinking about their meaning. In this chapter, we're going to talk about types of numbers (or scales) and how they can be used in measurement. Measurement is a way to give meaning to numbers.

Numbers and Scales

First of all, in measurement numbers compose scales. There are four scales of measurement: nominal, ordinal, interval, and ratio (Stevens, 1946). Although each of these scales is represented by numbers, they are very different and cannot be used interchangeably. So it's very important that you understand these four measurement scales.

Nominal

Nominal measurement scales are used to name or label things or to depict categories. Nominal scales put things or people into categories. For example, when you responded to the latest U.S. census, you indicated your gender and that placed you into a category—male or female. At this point you may be asking yourself, So what? In measurement, it is important to know characteristics of things or people. When trying to count the number of people in the United States, the government often wants to know how many men and women there are, not just the number of total citizens in the United States. Being able to examine citizens by gender allows you to get a more accurate picture of the people you are trying to measure. Other nominal categories that are frequently taken into consideration in measurement include categories such as race or ethnicity, marital status, or region of the United States.

Your social security number also names you. No other person has your number. It is uniquely yours. Similarly, universities use an identification (ID) number to represent you. When a faculty member needs to access your academic records, they look up your ID number. It is easier and more accurate to identify you by your ID number than your name (how many Mary Smiths are there anyway?). Both your social security number and your ID number are "shorthand" for you. Both are nominal-level data.

It is important to note that nominal scales cannot be added, subtracted, multiplied, or divided. You just cannot manipulate them mathematically. You can assign a value to categories, for example, 1 for men and 2 for women or vice versa. Regardless what number they are assigned, you cannot mathematically manipulate these numbers. For example, you cannot add a man and a woman or add social security numbers and get anything meaningful. Therefore, it is imperative that you remember that nominal scales only name things. Don't try to mess with them mathematically.

Ordinal

Ordinal scales order or rank things. Every child knows that it is better to be chosen first for a team than to be chosen sixth or tenth. Whoever is doing the choosing has made a judgment and ranked the other children by some trait or ability. In this case, the child chosen first was most likely perceived as the most skilled (or most liked?). In our society, we are taught to strive to be number one. We don't know how much better we are than number two, but we know we came in first. In measurement, an assigned rank given to a person or thing is an ordinal number.

While ordinal scales can be mathematically manipulated, special formulas are often required, and interpreting the findings is done with great care. One reason for this is that the differences between ranks can be very uneven. For example, let's pretend you are a fifth-grade teacher and you have to pick three students to compete in the school spelling bee. You have two dynamite spellers whom you quickly choose as your first and second choice—Nicole and Kevin. Sadly, the rest of your class is "spelling challenged." You pick the

```
┌─────────────────────────────────────────────────────────────────────┐
│ Spelling                                                              │
│ Challenged      Sarah                              Kevin Nicole       │
│ IIIIIIIIIII II II I____I_____I____I____        │
│                                                    Best Spellers      │
└─────────────────────────────────────────────────────────────────────┘
```

best of this group, and Sarah becomes your third spelling bee contestant. While there is minimal difference between Nicole and Kevin, Sarah is a long way behind them. These differences are not reflected in their ranks of 1, 2, and 3. Therefore, when your measurement data are ordinal, make any interpretations cautiously.

Interval

The most commonly used scale in measurement in the social sciences is the *interval scale*. Interval measurement scales are based on a continuum where the interval (or distance) between any two numbers is always the same. The intervals are equal to each other. Intervals can be any size, but in measurement the interval often is set at the unit 1. For example, if we were to give Nicole, Kevin, and Sarah a 100-word spelling test and their scores were 98 for Nicole, 97 for Kevin, and 80 for Sarah, we can say exactly how much higher Nicole scored than did Kevin (1 point) and Sarah (18 points).

Other times, however, the interval is set to include smaller pieces of information. Everyone knows that 1 inch contains smaller measurements, such as 1/2 inch, 1/4 inch, or 1/8 inch. All of us report our height in feet and inches and often in parts of inches. On a spelling test, however, you can't get half a word right. But, if you are taking an essay test, your professor may award you part of a point for getting close to the answer (at least we hope professors look on your ideas with a generous spirit).

Interval measurement scales can be manipulated mathematically to produce meaningful results. For example, in this class you're going to take a couple of tests, at least a midterm and a final. Your professor can calculate the average for the midterm and for the final for the entire class and compare your midterm and final scores to the class average for each test. Your professor also can calculate your average across the two tests. Each of these resulting numbers has meaning. Let's say you got 78 out of 100 possible points on your midterm. The mean for the class was 82. Realizing you needed to study harder, you pulled 92 out of 100 possible points on your final, and the class average for the final was 86 (we assumed almost everyone studied harder). You scored 4 points below the class average on the midterm ($82 - 78 = 4$) and 6 points above the class average on the final ($92 - 86 = 6$). The class average across the two tests was 84 [$(82 + 86)/2 = 84$] and your average was 85 [(78 +

92)/2 = 85]. Your average score was only 1 point (85 – 84 = 1) above the class average for the course.

As you can see, interval scores make sense when they are added, subtracted, multiplied, or divided. Knowing this, please, please study harder for your midterm.

Ratio

The most advanced, the most sophisticated, the most precise measurement scale is the *ratio scale*. The ratio measurement scale is distinguished from the interval measurement scale by the fact that it has an absolute, true zero that has meaning. An absolute zero means there is nothing present of the variable that is being measured. Death is the absolute absence of a life force. It is a true zero, even though Billy Crystal in *The Princess Bride* proclaimed the hero as "mostly dead." Other than death when studying people, it is rare to have an absolute zero in the social sciences.

Less interesting (we think) textbooks provide examples of zero-degree temperature and zero distance as absolute zeros on temperature and distance scales. We offer the example of a 100-word vocabulary assignment, and you have not learned one word. This is an absolute zero *with respect to the assignment* (and may reflect your grade if you don't get going). In the ratio scale, every measurement unit is equal. So if you learn the meaning of 50 words, you're halfway there.

The social sciences seldom use ratio scales since an absolute zero is so difficult to define. As Salkind (2004) pointed out, "Even if you score a 0 on that spelling test or miss every item on an IQ test (in Russian), it does not mean that you have no spelling ability or no intelligence" (p. 277). Similarly, even if you score 0 on the vocabulary test, this doesn't mean you have no vocabulary.

Like interval scales, ratio measurement scales can be mathematically manipulated and yield meaningful results. Using the vocabulary assignment above, you ended up memorizing 81 words and five of your classmates each memorized 100 words, and one person didn't do the assignment (absolute zero). The class memorized an average of 83 words [(81 + 100 + 100 + 100 + 100 + 100 + 0)/7 = 83]. The person who didn't do the assignment lowered the class average. The real advantage of a ratio scale is that you can accurately say things such as something is "twice as much" or "half as much."

Some Final Thoughts About Scales of Measurement

Scales of measurement are not all the same. They vary from simply naming a variable (nominal scales) to being able to provide information (interval and ratio scales) that can be mathematically manipulated. We use nominal scales to label people or things. In the behavioral or social sciences we most frequently use interval and ordinal measurement scales, because they are a good fit for the kind of information or numbers (also called *data*) that are used in the behavioral or social sciences. Ratio scales have a very stringent requirement—they must have a true zero. Even though we used exam scores as one of our examples to explain ratio scales, having absolutely no knowledge of what is being tested would be most unusual. Knowing absolutely nothing would be a true zero only with respect to this one test. In some ways, we have created an artificial "true" zero. (Can you really create something that's artificially true? As we said in our introduction, we're the good witches, so we have this power.)

To help you remember these four measurement scales, let's consider the following example. As a student you have a very limited budget. But you and your roommate eat peanut-butter-and-jelly sandwiches for a semester so you can go to Europe for 1 month during the summer. You buy a travel guidebook that classifies restaurants as $ (Cheap), $$ (Moderate), or $$$ (Expensive). This is ordinal level data and gives you a general idea of cost. Common sense tells you that you'll probably get your best meals at a $$$ restaurant, next best at $$ restaurant, and stave off hunger at the $ restaurant. Quality of meal is also ordinal data. Since you have to budget your money, it would be much more helpful if the guidebook had given actual prices (interval or ratio data) for each of these three classifications. If you spend no money on food, you automatically have a true zero (and will probably starve). Considering that the monetary unit (e.g., Euros) is a counting unit with equal intervals between amounts, you can divide your money so that you can eat at both cheap and expensive restaurants. Because money is a ratio scale, you can mathematically manipulate it.

 ## Let's Check Your Understanding

Before we introduce you to response formats, let's make sure you're getting the hang of this.

1. What is a nominal scale?

   _____

   _____

2. What is an ordinal scale?

   _____

   _____

3. What is an interval scale?

_____

_____

4. What is a ratio scale?

_____

_____

5. Which of these scales cannot be manipulated mathematically?

_____

_____

 ## Our Model Answers

1. What is a nominal scale?
   A nominal scale is used to name or label things or categories.

2. What is an ordinal scale?
   An ordinal scale orders or ranks things.

3. What is an interval scale?
   An interval scale presents a continuum of numbers where the interval between each number is equal.

4. What is a ratio scale?
   A ratio scale is an interval scale with an absolute true zero.

5. Which of these scales cannot be manipulated mathematically?
   You cannot meaningfully mathematically manipulate nominal-level scales.

Numbers and Response Formats

When we're gathering measurement data, we ask questions and get answers. What types of answers are possible reflects a format for responding. For example, sometimes when we measure variables, we ask people to respond in their own words. We call these responses open-ended because people can say anything they wish to answer the question. Other times, we want specific answers, so we provide a series of possible answers for them to choose from. When we limit response options, the response formats are dichotomous or continuous. This allows us to mathematically manipulate their responses in order to understand patterns of responding across people.

Dichotomous Responses

Sometimes we like to corner people and ask them to make a choice between yes or no, black or white, good or bad, like me or not like me, or to report whether something is true about them. When we do this, the response format is *dichotomous*. There are only two choices. There is no middle ground.

Let's look at the following example to illustrate our point. An instrument frequently used to measure stress asks whether specific events have been experienced in the past month. Some of the events include having a flat tire, breaking up with a boyfriend or girlfriend, or visiting a doctor. Ryan, a college freshman who has had difficulty adjusting to college life and is thinking about quitting, goes to the student counseling center. He takes an academic stress scale and has to respond "yes" or "no" to each statement. Each item has a truly natural dichotomous response format because the event either did or didn't happen to Ryan in the past month.

Other tests also use a dichotomous response format, but the response options are not natural dichotomies; they are forced-choice dichotomies. For example, a well-known social support instrument asks questions such as "I rely on my friends for emotional support" and "My friends seek me out for companionship." The only response options you have to these two statements are "yes" or "no." In reality, more accurate responses would reflect gray areas between yes and no. Ryan tells his counselor that he relies on friends for emotional support sometimes but not always. Furthermore, some of his friends are fickle and may ask someone else to go out with them. The yes-or-no-response format doesn't allow for his friends' inconsistencies.

Continuous Responses (Likert Scales and Their Cousins)

In its simplest form, *continuous responses* allow for three or more choices that increase in value. Now, back to Ryan . . . Let's say you're still trying to pin Ryan down about his friends, but he is faster afoot than you are. You demand, "Do your friends seek you out for companionship?" Ryan says, "Some of the time." While this response is not as clean as "yes" or "no," it gives us more information about Ryan's social support system. The response

"Some of the time" is only one of multiple choices when a *Likert-type response format* is used.

Likert-type scales allow for a continuum of responses. Typically, they allow for five, seven, or nine responses. For example, you may be asked to what extent you agree with the statement, "It has been difficult for me to meet and make friends with other students." The five-point response format would range from:

Strongly Disagree	Disagree	Neutral	Agree	Strongly Agree
1	2	3	4	5

It is also possible that the five-point response format could range from:

Strongly Disagree	Disagree	Neutral	Agree	Strongly Agree
0	1	2	3	4

Both of these examples, regardless of the numerical values assigned, depict five-point Likert-type response formats.

The two end points are called anchors. The seven-point and nine-point response formats would have the same anchors, but the middle points frequently are not labeled. Other common anchors are "Not at all" and "Completely"; "Not at all" and "A great deal"; and "Never" and "All of the time." Sometimes the numerical values assigned to the responses range from 1 to 7 or 0 to 6 for a seven-point Likert-type scale. When a nine-point scale is used, the range may be 0 to 8 or 1 to 9. There is no rule about assigning of numerical values except that the numbers must be in the numerical order that produces a continuum and are ordinal-level data. Remember the goal is to make sense of the numbers.

Likert scale cousins typically leave out the middle choice, thus forming a forced-choice response. For example, the Rosenberg Self-Esteem Scale (1979) uses a four-point response format. The response options are:

Strongly Disagree	Disagree	Agree	Strongly Agree
1	2	3	4

If our good friend, Ryan, was also taking this test, he would have to choose among these four answers. No middle-of-the-road cop-outs would be allowed!

Some Final Thoughts About Response Formats

Response formats for assessment instruments typically take three forms: open-ended, dichotomous, and continuous. We are most interested in the latter two.

Snapshots

© 2005 by Sharon E. Robinson Kurpius, Mary E. Stafford, and Jason Love

Figure 1.1   Response Formats

- Dichotomous responses have only two options. "Open wide! It's your tooth or your pain" is a natural dichotomy even though you are forced to make a choice between your tooth and your pain. If you don't answer, the dentist may ask, "How bad is your pain anyway?" Your response, "On a scale of 1 to 7, my pain is about 5," reflects a continuous response format.

- Continuous responses add texture and allow shades of gray interpretations.
- Both dichotomous and continuous responses can be mathematically manipulated to yield interesting information about people or things being measured.

Let's Check Your Understanding

1. Dichotomous response format allows for _____ response options.

2. The two types of dichotomous response formats are _____ and _____.

3. A response format that allows for more than two choices is _____.

4. A Likert-type response format is a _____ response format.

5. The most typical number of Likert response options are _____, _____, and _____.

6. A typical set of anchors for Likert response options might be _____ and _____.

Our Model Answers

1. Dichotomous response format allows for **two** response options.

2. The two types of dichotomous response formats are **natural dichotomies** and **forced dichotomies.**

3. A response format that allows for more than two choices is **continuous.**

4. A Likert-type response format is a **continuous** response format.

5. The most typical number of Likert response options are **5, 7, and 9.**

6. A typical set of anchors for Likert response options might be **strongly disagree and strongly agree. Other anchor pairs might include "not at all" to "completely"; "never" to "all the time"; or "not at all" to "a great deal."**

Numbers and Test Scores—How Do They Relate?

In case you weren't paying attention when you read "A Note to Students" at the beginning of this book, let's review what a test is. A *test* is a sample of behavior or characteristic at a given point in time. For the purposes of this book, we are interested in measurement concepts related to test scores that are numerical. Measurement of open-ended responses presents a completely different set of issues beyond the scope of this book. Sorry, but we won't be discussing them, even though they can be very enlightening.

It's time to tie the ideas in this chapter together to solidify your understanding. These ideas are the building blocks for the rest of this book. First, when taking a test, people are expected to respond in some way. While we are interested in dichotomous or continuous response formats, we are absolutely fascinated with total test scores and their characteristics. You're probably thinking right now, "They need to get a life!"

To prove to you how interesting total test scores can be, let's revisit Ryan. A counselor at the student counseling center gave Ryan an instrument to measure stress. He had to respond "yes" (scored 1) or "no" (scored 0) to each statement on the instrument. When all his "yes" responses are added, his total score, which is interval-level data, is a reflection of the accumulation of stressful events in Ryan's life. Theory tells us the more stressful events that occur in a short time period, the more likely the individual, in this case Ryan, is to report feeling stressed. Being caring, empathic people, of course we are concerned about our friend Ryan feeling stressed and we don't want him to quit school. The counselor can look at Ryan's total stress score and then at individual items to target areas to help Ryan cope with college life better.

Ryan also took a social support instrument that had a forced dichotomy response format. In spite of the response format being forced, Ryan's total score reflects his perceptions of social support. This total score is interval-level data that can be mathematically played with and tells the counselor whether Ryan needs to work on expanding his social network.

Total scores from the social support and stress instruments are interval-level data. Even if someone answered "no" to every item on each test, this would not be interpreted as an absolute absence of social support or stress. On both tests, scores of 0 do NOT reflect an absolute zero with respect to the constructs stress and social support.

See, we told you total test scores could be interesting. Hopefully, by the end of this class, you too will be interested in test scores and their measurement. A few of you may even become fascinated.☺

Some Final Thoughts About Measurement Scales and Response Formats

Test responses can form nominal, ordinal, interval, or, on rare occasion, ratio scales. Depending on what you're trying to find out, you will choose questions or tests that give you the type of data that best answers your questions. Remember the U.S. census? If you wanted to know the racial or ethnic minority population in the United States, what type of scale do you want? THAT'S RIGHT—Nominal! Next, if you wanted to rank racial or ethnic minority groups from the largest to the smallest, what type of scale do you want? Before you jump to an answer, look at the question again. The key words are *largest* and *smallest*. These words key you that we are going to look at order; therefore, you want an ordinal scale. Finally, if you wanted to know the actual numerical size of the largest and smallest racial or ethnic minority group, what type of scale do you want? Hint: Two answers are possible. Both interval and ratio level scales would provide you with meaningful numbers that would allow you to give exact sizes. You could even calculate the difference in number of people between the largest and smallest racial or ethnic minority groups (as well as all of the groups between the largest and smallest). As an aside, ratio would be the best answer if every single racial or ethnic minority person in the United States had completed the census, since that would allow us an absolute zero. Being realists, we realize that not everyone completed the census. Therefore, the most appropriate scale is interval.

For each of the three census questions above, we used numbers and scales to arrive at meaningful answers. That is what testing is all about—using numbers that are appropriate for the issues being addressed to arrive at information that can guide our decisions and behaviors. Knowing that this information is actually going to impact your decisions and what you do, you want these numbers to be as accurate and truthful as possible.

Key Terms

To help you review the information presented in this chapter, you need to understand and be able to explain the following concepts. If you are not sure, look back and reread.

- Test
- Measurement scales
  - Nominal scale
  - Ordinal scale
  - Interval scale
  - Ratio scale

- Response format
  - Dichotomous response format (natural or forced)
  - Continuous response format
- Anchors
- Total score

Models and Self-instructional Exercises

Our goal is to have you master the concepts we presented and to use the concepts appropriately in answering questions or solving problems related to measurement. In this chapter, which presented some basic measurement concepts, we gave you lots of examples to illustrate these concepts. Before we see what you've learned, we're going to model for you how to use the concepts we just introduced and then give you a chance to practice. When reading our model, try to answer the questions before you look at our answers.

Our Model

The process of transitioning from high school to college is difficult for many students. One factor that eases this transition is becoming involved on campus. As a student affairs employee at ABC University, you are charged with finding out why some students dropped out (nonpersisters) and some stayed enrolled (persisters).

1. If you grouped students by their persistence, what kind of scale have you created?

   _____

   _____

2. If you asked them whether they lived on-campus, off-campus, or with family, what kind of scale would you have?

   _____

   _____

3. You asked them whether or not they had joined a variety of activities on campus, and they answered yes ("1") or no ("0").
   a. What kind of response format is this?

   _____

   _____

   b. When you add up their responses, what kind of scale are you creating?

   _____

   _____

4. If you have them respond on a five-point Likert scale as to how involved they are in each activity they belong to, what kind of scale are you creating?

_____

_____

Our Model Answers

1. If you grouped students by their persistence, what kind of scale have you created?

   You have created a nominal scale with two categories: persisters and nonpersisters.

2. If you asked them whether they live on-campus, off-campus, or with family, what kind of scale would you have?

   Surprise, you still have a nominal scale—with three categories this time.

3. You asked them whether or not they had joined a variety of activities on campus, and they answered yes ("1") or no ("0").
   a. What kind of response format is this?

      This is a dichotomous response format.
   b. When you add up their responses, what kind of scale are you creating?

      You are creating a ratio scale, because there is a true zero if they belong to no campus activities.

4. If you have them respond on a five-point Likert scale as to how involved they are in each activity they belong to, what kind of scale are you creating?

   You are creating an ordinal scale.

Now It's Your Turn

Too many American children are becoming addicted to tobacco at an early age. National data tell us that age of first experimentation with cigarettes is between 9 and 11 years old. This is a grave concern because earlier initial use is directly linked to stronger addiction and serious health complications as adults. As measurement specialists, you are asked to assess cigarette use in a large metropolitan school district (they will even pay you). You decide to administer the Adolescent At-Risk Behaviors Inventory (Robinson, 1992), not only to look at tobacco use but also to provide the school district with information about other at-risk behaviors. One series of questions asks the students whether they have tried tobacco or cigarettes, alcohol, and/or other drugs. A second series of questions asks about frequency of use, with response choices being never, sometimes, often, and frequently. A third set of questions asks students to indicate how many cigarettes they smoke each day and each week. They were given six response options ranging from no cigarettes per day, 1 to 4 cigarettes per day, 5 to 8, 9 to 12, 13 to 16, and 17 to a full pack (20 cigarettes) per day. This question is paralleled with questions about drug and alcohol use. Based on these test questions, you are able to classify kids as smokers or nonsmokers, alcohol users or nonusers, and drug users or nonusers.

1. When students indicate whether or not they use tobacco or cigarettes (or alcohol or drugs):
   a. What type of response format is being used?

   _____

   _____

   b. Why would you choose to use this response format?

   _____

   _____

   c. What type of measurement scale is being used?

   _____

   _____

2. You would also like to be able to determine whether or not each student is "at-risk" for substance use. Substance use is defined as use of tobacco or cigarettes and/or alcohol and/or drugs.
   a. How would you go about creating dichotomous categories for substance use?

   _____

   _____

   b. Is this a natural or forced dichotomy and why?

   _____

   _____

3. Although in reality use of tobacco or cigarettes, alcohol, and drugs is not equivalent in terms of at-risk behaviors, for the sake of our measurement questions, let's pretend it is. Using this assumption,
   a. How would you create a scale that would rank order at-risk behaviors from "not at risk" to "high risk"? (Here is a hint: The lowest rank, "not at risk," would reflect no at-risk behaviors related to substance use.)

_____

_____

b. What type of measurement scale have you created?

_____

_____

4. The second series of questions about frequency of use has
   a. What type of response format?

_____

_____

b. This response format reflects what type of measurement scale?

_____

_____

5. If we assigned a 0 to "never," a 1 to "sometimes," a 2 to "often," and a 3 to "frequently," we have created what kind of measurement scale?

_____

_____

6. The most specific data are provided in the questions asking how many cigarettes they smoke each day and each week. Using these questions,
   a. What type of response format is used?

_____

_____

b. What kind of measurement scale was created?

_____

_____

 ## Our Model Answers

Now it is time to see if you have started thinking like measurement specialists. Come on now, that's not a bad thing. Below are model answers to each of the questions we asked you to solve. Compare your answers to ours and pat yourself on the back when you are right. Don't feel badly if you aren't right. This is still a learning experience. Look at our answer and modify your thinking, so next time you'll arrive at the correct answer too.

1. When students indicate whether or not they use tobacco or cigarettes (or alcohol or drugs):

   a. What type of response format is being used?

   Dichotomous response format is being used.

   b. Why would you choose to use this response format?

   A dichotomous response format was chosen because we were only interested in whether tobacco or cigarettes were used (yes) or not (no). Similarly, we are only interested in whether or not alcohol or drugs were used.

   c. What type of measurement scale is being used?

   A nominal measurement scale is being used because we are categorizing students as smokers or nonsmokers (or alcohol users or nonusers, or drug users or nonusers). We have named them.

2. You would also like to be able to determine whether or not each student is "at-risk" for substance use. *Substance use* is defined as use of tobacco or cigarettes and/or alcohol and/or drugs.

   a. How would you go about creating dichotomous categories for substance use?

   First, you want to create two categories. For clarity name them "substance use" and "substance nonuse." Then, if a student answered "yes" to any of the questions that asked whether or not they used tobacco or cigarettes, alcohol, or drugs, the student will be placed in the "substance use" category. If they answered "no" to all three questions, they are placed in the "substance nonuse" category.

   b. Is this a natural or forced dichotomy and why?

   This is a forced dichotomy because whether the student used just one substance or two substances or all three, he or she was placed in the "substance use" category.

3. Although in reality use of tobacco or cigarettes, alcohol, and drugs is not equivalent in terms of at-risk behaviors, for the sake of our measurement questions, let's pretend it is. Using this assumption,

   a. How would you create a scale that would rank order at-risk behaviors from "not at risk" to "high risk"? Here is a hint: The lowest rank, "not at risk," would reflect no at-risk behaviors related to substance use.

   First, to answer this question you have to look at the response options for each of the three substances. If students answer "no" to all three questions about whether they use each substance, they would be placed in the "not at risk" category. If they reported using

one of the three substances, they would be placed in a next higher category, which might be labeled "somewhat at risk." If they reported using two of the three substances, they would be placed in an even higher category, which might be labeled "moderately at risk." Finally, if they reported using all three substances, they would be placed in the highest at-risk category, labeled "high risk." Voila, you have successfully created graduated categories of substance use.

   b. What type of measurement scale have you created?

   The measurement scale is ordinal because it is on a continuum of increased usage without the amount of usage being taken into consideration.

4. The second series of questions about frequency of use has
   a. What type of response format?

   This is a continuous response format because there are four response options that fall along a continuum from never to frequently.

   b. This response format reflects what type of measurement scale?

   This reflects an ordinal measurement scale because it reflects qualitative differences in frequency of use but does not specify exact differences between the four response options.

5. If we assigned a 0 to "never," a 1 to "sometimes," a 2 to "often," and a 3 to "frequently," we have created what kind of measurement scale?

   We have created a Likert-type scale with the assumption of *interval* equivalence for both labels and their assigned numbers.

6. The most specific data are provided in the questions asking how many cigarettes they smoke each day and each week. Using these questions,
   a. What type of response format is used?

   Students were given six response options ranging from no cigarettes each day to up to 17 to 20 cigarettes per day. These response options reflect a Likert-type (continuous) response format.

   b. What kind of measurement scale was created?

   Because some students smoke no cigarettes (absolute zero) and because the other responses are continuous, the measurement scale is ratio level.

 ## Words of Encouragement

Phew!!! What a challenge that was! But by now you are experts on response formats and measurement scales. And even more important, you've started to use this knowledge to address measurement problems. Congratulations!! You've come a long way in a short time period.☺

CHAPTER 2

Frequencies: One Potato, Two Potato, Three Potato, Four

In the first chapter, you've learned about some basic measurement principles: measurement scales and response formats. It's time to step up your learning another level. Don't worry; it's only a small step. Besides that, we're right here to catch you and bolster your learning.

The new topic is *frequencies* and *frequency distributions*. The chapter title—"One Potato, Two Potato, Three Potato, Four"—reflects frequency data. The variable being examined is potatoes, and we have four of them (the frequency count). Now, we know you're not interested in potatoes, but what if you were counting money? Imagine that you just discovered a chest full of currency in your grandmother's basement. Wouldn't you like to know how much is there? An easy way to find out is to divide the bills by denomination (i.e., $1, $5, $10, $20, $50, and $100) and count how many of each you have. Surprise, you have just done the rudiments of creating a frequency distribution, a simple method of organizing data.

A *frequency distribution* presents scores (X) and how many times (f) each score was obtained. Relative to tests and measurement, frequency distributions present scores and how many individuals received each score. There are three types of frequency distributions—ungrouped, grouped, and cumulative.

Ungrouped Frequency Distributions

An *ungrouped frequency distribution*, most often referred to as just plain old frequency distribution, lists every possible score individually. The *scores*, which are typically designated by a capital "X," are listed in numerical order. In a column paralleling the X scores is a column that indicates how many people got the corresponding X score. In this column, which is designated by a small "*f*," the frequencies are recorded. Sometimes the frequencies are presented as tally marks, and sometimes they are presented as numbers.

Let's go back to your measurement midterm where you scored 78 out of 100 points. For our illustration, let's say one poor soul really messed up and scored only 56, the lowest score on the test. One very bright (or very lucky) person scored a perfect 100. There are 25 people in your class. "*N*" is used to represent the number of people in the entire distribution. Table 2.1 presents what the frequency distribution of everyone's midterm scores looks like.

Table 2.1   Frequency Distribution of Midterm Grades

Score X	f	Score X	f
100	1	77	
99		76	
98	1	75	1
97		74	
96		73	1
95	1	72	
94		71	1
93	2	70	
92		69	
91		68	
90	2	67	
89	1	66	
88		65	
87	2	64	
86	1	63	
85	3	62	
84		61	
83	1	60	
82		59	
81	2	58	
80	2	57	
79	1	56	1
78	1		

$$N = 25$$

By creating this frequency distribution, we can get a bird's eye view of the class's performance on the midterm. The numbers in the "*f*" column indicate how many students received each score. For example, three people earned an 85, and you were the Lone Ranger at 78. Looking at these data, you can also create a cumulative frequency column that would tell you how many people scored lower than or equal to you. Don't worry! We'll explain cumulative frequencies later.

Before we leave ungrouped frequency distributions, however, we feel obliged to point out some of their shortcomings. As you can see from

Table 2.1, the score range may be really large (in this case from 56 to 100), and the frequency distribution gets stretched out. This is not very efficient, although it is very accurate. The most important shortcoming, however, is that often no one gets some of the possible scores. This makes the frequency distribution more difficult to interpret.

For those of you who like to use statistical programs to look at data, we have run the SPSS (Statistical Packages for the Social Sciences) statistical program for frequencies using the midterm scores for this group of 25 people. We gave each person an identification number (nominal-level data) from 1 to 25 and then gave each person his or her midterm test score (interval level data). Next, we clicked on Analyze. Under Analyze, we chose Descriptive Statistics and then chose Frequencies. We asked for them to be presented in descending order. The printout looks like Table 2.2.

Table 2.2   SPSS Printout of Frequency Distribution of Midterm Grades

		Midterm Grades			
		Frequency	Percent	Valid Percent	Cumulative Percent
Valid	100	1	4.0	4.0	4.0
	98	1	4.0	4.0	8.0
	95	1	4.0	4.0	12.0
	93	2	8.0	8.0	20.0
	90	2	8.0	8.0	28.0
	89	1	4.0	4.0	32.0
	87	2	8.0	8.0	40.0
	86	1	4.0	4.0	44.0
	85	3	12.0	12.0	56.0
	83	1	4.0	4.0	60.0
	81	2	8.0	8.0	68.0
	80	2	8.0	8.0	76.0
	79	1	4.0	4.0	80.0
	78	1	4.0	4.0	84.0
	75	1	4.0	4.0	88.0
	73	1	4.0	4.0	92.0
	71	1	4.0	4.0	96.0
	56	1	4.0	4.0	100.0
	Total	25	100.0	100.0	

Notice that SPSS ignored all scores that were not obtained by anyone. This makes the printout more efficient, but it also requires you to pay close attention to the actual values that people received. In addition, the SPSS printout provides you with percentages and cumulative percentages. Ignore these for now.

Grouped Frequency Distributions

To be more economical or efficient, scores also can be clustered into grouped frequency distributions. When scores are spread over a wide range, the use of a *grouped frequency distribution* is appropriate. Scores are collapsed into *class intervals* that are *mutually exclusive*. Mutually exclusive means that a score belongs to one and only one class interval. There is no swinging back and forth. A *class interval* is a grouping of scores. For each data set, all class intervals have the same width. The *width*, depicted by "*i*," is the range of scores for each group. Now, we bet that this is about as clear as mud to you. An example might help you see what we're talking about.

If a class interval width is set at 5 ($i = 5$) and the highest score possible is 75, the highest class interval would include scores from 71 to 75. Specifically, the five scores (71, 72, 73, 74, and 75) that compose the range have been collapsed into this class interval "71–75." What do you think the next lowest class interval would be? Remember it needs to contain the next lowest five scores when counting down. . . . OK. The answer is 66–70. To check yourself, ask these two questions: Have you included five numbers in the class interval and is this interval mutually exclusive from the one above it? Now just for fun, what would the next lower class interval be? THAT'S RIGHT. . . it's 61–65.

Now you understand the concepts of width, class interval, and mutual exclusivity. We should tell you, however, that we don't arbitrarily pick a width when we want to group our data. A rule of thumb for creating group distributions is to aim for 15 class intervals. Based on your data, however, the number of class intervals might range anywhere from 10 to 20. The number of class intervals you want will determine the size of your width.

In the example we just did, possible scores ranged from 1 to 75. Based on this information, there is a down and dirty way to calculate the appropriate class interval width. First, subtract the lowest possible score (in this case 1) from the highest (in this case 75) and then add 1, that is, $(75 - 1) + 1 = 75$. Then you divide by the number of class intervals you want, ideally 15, that is, $75/15 = 5$. The resulting number is the width of your class interval or the number of scores that compose each interval. In our example, we assumed that people obtained scores that reflect the entire possible range (i.e., someone scored in the 70s and someone scored 5 or below). When the range is much smaller, you can use the highest score earned and the lowest score earned to calculate your class interval.

Let's apply these principles to your class's midterm test scores. First, let's figure out the difference between the highest score earned (100) and the lowest score earned (56), and then add one point. The answer is 45. This is what you did, depicted mathematically: $[(100 - 56) + 1 = 45]$. If we aim for 15 class intervals, we'll divide 45 by 15. The answer, 3, is the width of each class interval if we are going to have 15 class intervals. So far, so good?

Now let's create our class intervals, starting with the highest class interval. The largest number is the largest score earned, 100. You count down so your class interval contains three numbers. Remember you want three numbers because your class interval width is 3. Therefore, the numbers included would be 100, 99, and 98. You would present these as 98–100 in your grouped frequency distribution. If you go down three more numbers, you will have 95–97. Your entire distribution is presented in Table 2.3.

Table 2.3   Grouped Frequency Distribution of Midterm Grades

Class Interval	f
98–100	2
95–97	1
92–94	2
89–91	3
86–88	3
83–85	4
80–82	4
77–79	2
74–76	1
71–73	2
68–70	
65–67	
62–64	
59–61	
56–58	1
$N = 25$	$i = 3$

Once you have grouped possible scores, you can determine into which score range your classmates most frequently fell. In this case, an equal number of people (four to be exact) scored between 80 and 82 and between 83 and 85. You can say that roughly a third of your class scored between 80 and 85, since eight of your 25 classmates were in this range.

Although you won't need to know this until you reach Chapter 5 on standardized scores, class intervals have what are called their limits. The *upper limit* (*UL*) is that point halfway between the value of the highest number in that interval and the value of the lowest number in the interval above it. For example, for the interval 66–70, the *UL* is the point halfway between this interval and the one above it (71–75). This number is derived by averaging 70 (highest point in the 66–70 interval) and

71 (the lowest point in the 71–75 interval). The *UL* for 66–70 is 70.5. When finding the *lower limit* (*LL*), you do just the same process, with the exception that you find the point halfway between the value of the lowest number in that interval containing your score and the value of the highest number in the interval below it. For the interval 66–70, you would take the average of 66 and 65 (highest value of the 61–65 interval). The *LL* for the 66–70 interval is 65.5.

Let's Check Your Understanding

Enough of simple frequency distributions! It's time to check your understanding.

1. What is an ungrouped frequency distribution?

   _____

   _____

2. What is a grouped frequency distribution?

   _____

   _____

3. What do the following symbols represent?
   a. X

   _____

   _____

   b. i

   _____

   _____

   c. UL

   _____

   _____

   d. LL

   _____

   _____

4. As a "rule of thumb," how many class intervals are typically created for a set of data?

_____

_____

5. When we say class intervals are mutually exclusive, what do we mean by mutually exclusive?

_____

_____

 Our Model Answers

1. What is an ungrouped frequency distribution?

   An ungrouped frequency distribution presents individual scores (X) and how many times (f) each score was obtained.

2. What is a grouped frequency distribution?

   A grouped frequency distribution presents scores collapsed into class intervals and how many times scores in each interval were obtained.

3. What do the following symbols represent?

   a. X

   X represents scores.

   b. i

   i represents the width of the class interval.

   c. UL

   UL represents the upper limit of the class interval.

   d. LL

   LL represents the lower limit of the class interval.

4. As a "rule of thumb," how many class intervals are typically created for a set of data?

   We typically aim for 15 class intervals when creating grouped frequency distributions.

5. When we say class intervals are mutually exclusive, what do we mean by mutually exclusive?

   Mutually exclusive means that a score belongs to one and only one class interval.

Cumulative Frequency Distribution

Often, it is desirable to calculate the *cumulative frequency distribution* from a set of data. The *cumulative frequency*, denoted *cf*, is the number of people who score at or below a particular class interval. It is calculated by adding the frequency associated with a single score (for ungrouped data) or with a class interval (for grouped data) to the number of cases or frequencies below that score or class interval. Cumulative frequency allows you to see where you score in relation to others.

To calculate cumulative frequencies, you start by adding frequencies for the lowest score "*X*" for simple frequency data, or for the lowest class interval for grouped data, to the frequencies above. For our example in Table 2.3, the lowest class interval is 56–58, so that is where we'll start adding. The number in the *cf* column indicates the number of students who have scored in or below that class interval. If no one scored in that class interval, you repeat the number below (in reality, you have added 0 to the *cf* for the class interval below). A way to check the accuracy of your *cf* is to make sure that the highest *cf* is exactly equal to the number of people who took the test or who were being measured in some way.

As they say, a picture is worth a thousand words. So, follow the example in Table 2.4.

Table 2.4   Cumulative Frequency Distribution of Midterm Grades

Class Interval	f	cf
98–100	2	25
95–97	1	23
92–94	2	22
89–91	3	20
86–88	3	17
83–85	4	14
80–82	4	10
77–79	2	6
74–76	1	4
71–73	2	3
68–70		1
65–67		1
62–64		1
59–61		1
56–58	1	1
N = 25		*i* = 3

Hopefully you can see that the cumulative frequency is arrived at simply by adding the numbers in the corresponding frequency column (f) to the cumulative frequency (cf) below. For example, if you wanted to know the cumulative frequency of the class interval 89–91, you would add the three people in 89–91 to the 17 who scored below that interval. Your answer is 20. But what does this 20 mean? It means that 20 people scored at or below 91 (which is the largest number in that class interval) on their midterm exam. The cf for the 74–76 class interval is arrived at by summing the 1 person (f) in this interval with the 3 in the cf column below this interval. The resulting cf is 4. Four people scored at or below 76 (the highest number in the 74–76 class interval).

Now, you tell us, how did we arrive at a cumulative frequency of 14 for the 83–85 class interval? . . . THAT'S RIGHT! First, we looked at the frequency for the class interval 83–85, and find that four people scored between 83 and 85. Then we look at the cf for the class interval just below the 83–85 class interval. The cf was 10. To determine the cf in the 83–85 class interval, we added the f for the 83–85 class interval ($f = 4$) to the cf of 10 in the class interval below it. And we arrive at an answer of 14.

OK, let's do another example using the data in Table 2.4. How did we arrive at the cf of 1 for the 59–61 class interval? . . . If you said to yourself, "No one scored in this interval," you're right! If we had placed an f value next to this class interval, it would have been a 0. But the accepted convention is not to put 0 frequencies into the table. This leaves you with the task of remembering that an empty f means 0 and then you have to add this 0 to the cf below. So, mentally, we added 0 to 1 to arrive at the cf of 1 for the 59–61 class interval. As a matter of fact, we kept adding 0 to the cf of 1 until we reached the class interval of 71–73 that actually had two people represented in its f column.

Some Final Thoughts About Frequency Distributions

You may be asking yourself, "Now that I've learned this, what am I going to do with it?" As we said earlier, frequency distributions give you a "bird's eye view" of your measurement data. A test score, in and of itself, is meaningless. It takes on meaning only when you are able to compare it to other scores. Frequency distributions are one of the easiest and simplest ways to compare scores. In fact,

- Frequency distributions are an initial step to ordering and making sense out of test scores.
- Frequency distributions provide a visual representation of how individuals scored.

- Grouped frequency distributions allow you to collapse very spread out data into a more efficient and economical form that is easier to understand.
- Cumulative frequency distributions allow you to see where you score in relation to others on an individual test.

Key Terms

To help you review the information presented in this chapter, you need to understand and be able to explain the following concepts. If you are not sure, look back and reread.

- Frequency
- Score
- Frequency distributions
  - Ungrouped
  - Grouped
  - Cumulative
- Class interval
- Upper limit of a class interval (*UL*)
- Lower limit of a class interval (*LL*)
- Width
- Mutually exclusive

Models and Self-instructional Exercises

Here we are again. We're going to model how to use the concepts just introduced and then give you a chance to practice. Remember, when reading our model, try to answer the questions before you look at our model answers.

Our Model

The College Stress Scale, an instrument that measures perceived stress, consists of 30 items and has a five-point Likert response format. (Just checking to make sure you haven't forgotten concepts you learned in Chapter 1.) The possible score range is from 30 to 150. We got that by multiplying 30 (items) times 1 (the lowest response possible for each item) and 30 (items) times 5 (the highest response possible for each item). The higher the overall score, the greater the perceived stress. Remember our unhappy college freshman, Ryan? If he had answered all 1s, he would have gotten a 30 (but we may not believe that he was very truthful in his answers). If he had answered all

5s, he would have scored 150 (if he has that much stress in his life, we are going to rush him to the Student Health Center immediately before he has a nervous breakdown or heart attack). In actuality, Ryan scored 92. Thirty-nine other freshmen also took this stress test at the counseling center. We are interested in how perceived college stress is distributed throughout this group of freshmen and how Ryan compares to other freshmen.

Here are the perceived college stress scores for all 40 freshmen.

36	86	104	83	56	62	69	77
92	39	110	80	58	84	74	80
52	54	93	60	88	67	46	72
53	68	73	73	81	62	99	69
65	80	71	79	49	78	64	85

In order to make sense of these scores, we first have to reorder them in descending order. The reordering would look like this:

110	88	81	78	72	67	60	52
104	86	80	77	71	65	58	49
99	85	80	74	69	64	56	46
93	84	80	73	69	62	54	39
92	83	79	73	68	62	53	36

1. Create a grouped and cumulative distribution table using 15 class intervals. To do this, determine the following:
   a. What is the highest score received?

   _____

   b. What is the lowest score received?

   _____

   c. What is your interval size?

   _____

2. How many students are in the lowest class interval?

   _____

Class Interval	f	cf
N =		i =

3. How many students reported being more stressed than Ryan, based on the cumulative frequency distribution? (Remember, Ryan scored a 92.)

_____

 ## Our Model Answers

1. Create a grouped and cumulative distribution table using 15 class intervals. To do this, determine the following:
   a. What is the highest score received?
      The highest score received is 110.
   b. What is the lowest score received?
      The lowest score received is 36.
   c. What is your interval size?
      The interval size is 5. We arrived at this answer by subtracting 36 from 110 and adding 1 and then dividing by 15.

$$i = \frac{110 - 36 + 1}{15} = 5$$

Class Interval	f	cf
106–110	1	40
101–105	1	39
96–100	1	38
91–95	2	37
86–90	2	35
81–85	4	33
76–80	6	29
71–75	5	23
66–70	4	18
61–65	4	14
56–60	3	10
51–55	3	7
46–50	2	4
41–45		2
36–40	2	2
$N = 40$		$i = 5$

2. How many students are in the lowest class interval?

   2

3. How many students reported being more stressed than Ryan, based on the cumulative frequency distribution?

   Three students were in the class intervals above the interval that contains Ryan's score. We can tentatively conclude that compared to his peers, Ryan is stressed about college, even though we wouldn't immediately rush him to the Student Health Center.

Now It's Your Turn

We know that social support is a buffer to protect against the ill effects of stress. Ryan and his peers also completed a social support scale. There are 20 items that are answered either "yes," "not sure," or "no." "No" responses receive zero points, "not sure" responses receive one point, and "yes" responses receive two points. This is a three-point Likert-type response format. The possible range of scores for this social support scale is 0 to 40, with higher scores reflecting more perceived social support. Ryan's score is 15. Scores for all 40 freshmen follow.

21	20	22	30	22	27	19	24
24	15	24	15	18	24	11	23
16	25	16	29	17	25	20	26
29	23	13	20	21	22	21	20
27	27	18	21	25	20	18	28

1. Reorder these scores in the table below in descending order.

2. Next, create a grouped and cumulative frequency distribution table by first determining the class interval width on the lines below. (Hint: You may want to use fewer than 15 intervals. We suggest 10.) Then, fill in the table below.

_____

_____

Class Interval	f	cf
$N =$	$i =$	

3. Determine the following:
   a. How many freshmen perceived that they have a poorer social support system than Ryan?

   _____

   b. How did you arrive at this number?

   _____

   _____

4. What would you conclude about Ryan's perception of his social support system?

   _____

   _____

   _____

 Our Model Answers

1. Reorder these scores in the table below in descending order.

30	27	25	23	21	20	18	16
29	27	24	23	21	20	18	15
29	26	24	22	21	20	18	15
28	25	24	22	21	20	17	13
27	25	24	22	20	19	16	11

2. Next, create a grouped and cumulative frequency distribution table by first determining the class interval width on the lines below. (Hint: You may want to use fewer than 15 intervals. We suggest 10.) Then, fill in the table below.

   First, for determining the class interval width: (30 − 11) + 1 = 20. Then 20 divided by 10 = 2. Thus, the width of the class intervals is 2. (See page 34 for the completed table.)

3. Determine the following:
   a. How many freshmen perceived that they have a poorer social support system than Ryan?
   Only 2 people.

Class Interval	f	cf
29–30	3	40
27–28	4	37
25–26	4	32
23–24	6	28
21–22	7	23
19–20	6	16
17–18	4	10
15–16	4	6
13–14	1	2
11–12	1	1
$N = 40$		$i = 2$

b. How did you arrive at this number?
We looked at the cumulative frequency below the class interval that contained Ryan's score of 15 (i.e., $cf = 2$ for class interval 13-14).

4. What would you conclude about Ryan's perception of his social support system?
As compared to the vast majority of his peers, Ryan does not believe he has a good, if any, social support system. Perhaps Ryan would benefit from social skills training.

Words of Encouragement

Congratulations! You have successfully completed almost 20% of the chapters in this book. If we're right, you now know some of the most basic measurement concepts. You have even started to demonstrate an ability to give meaning to test scores. We are proud of the progress you are making. Give yourself a pat on your back. If you want to challenge yourself further, go to www.sagepub.com/kurpius. We have provided you with larger SPSS data sets to play with and to test your understanding.

CHAPTER 3

The Distribution of Test Scores—The Perfect Body?

As we noted in Chapter 2, frequency distributions give you a bird's eye view of scores and allow you to make simple comparisons among the people who took your test. The problem with frequency distributions, however, is that they don't allow you to make really precise comparisons. To help you become slightly more sophisticated in your ability to compare test scores across people, we're going to teach you about *frequency curves.*

The first step in getting more meaning out of a frequency distribution is to graph it. This graph is called a frequency curve. A graph is created by two axes. Along the horizontal axis (*x*-axis), the score values are presented in ascending order. Along the vertical axis (*y*-axis), the frequency of people who could have gotten each score appears. Zero is the point where the *y*-axis intersects with the *x*-axis. For group frequency data, the possible intervals are listed on the *x*-axis. Although the midpoint score is typically used to represent the entire interval, in order not to confuse you, in our examples we will list the exact scores obtained within each interval.

Frequency curves can take on an unlimited number of shapes, but in measurement we most often assume that scores are distributed in a "bell-shaped" normal curve—the perfect body! This body is *symmetrical.* When you draw it, you can fold it in half and one side will be a reflection of the other.

Kurtosis

The normal curve also possesses a quality called kurtosis (no, that's not bad breath). *Kurtosis* is one aspect of how scores are distributed—how flat or how peaked. There are three forms of a normal curve depending on the distribution, or kurtosis, of scores. These forms are referred to as *mesokurtic, leptokurtic,* and *platykurtic* curves. Our friendly ghosts in Figure 3.1 illustrate these curves.

The first curve is the *mesokurtic curve.* While this is certainly not the perfect shape for the human body, it is the perfect body in measurement. It is what you typically think of as a normal, bell-shaped curve. Scores are nicely distributed around a clear central score. The majority of the scores fall in the center with fewer and fewer scores occurring as you move further from the center. The curve is just right—not too fat and not too skinny. We'll tell you a lot more about the normal curve when we discuss central tendencies and dispersion in the next chapter.

We all know, however, that it's rare to have a perfect body. A curve can be bell shaped and symmetrical, but be too skinny. This is called a *leptokurtic curve.* Almost everyone's scores cluster in the middle so that the bell-shaped curve is pointy and skinny. You can remember the name of this type of curve by thinking that the scores are leaping (lepto) up in the middle.

Figure 3.1   Kurtosis

A curve can also be too fat. A curve that is too fat is called a *platykurtic curve*. Instead of scores leaping up in one cluster, they have spread themselves out like melting butter. There is still a slightly higher middle point and the curve is still symmetrical, but scores are spread out rather evenly from the lowest to highest points. To help you remember a platykurtic normal curve, you can remember that "plat" rhymes with flat and fat. Or, if you have a good visual imagination, you might think of the flat-billed platypus and compare its bill to the rather flat platykurtic curve.

Each one of these three curves is *symmetrical*. For each, the two halves match. This means that half of the scores are in one half of the curve and half of the scores are in the other half of the curve. (You'll be glad we told you this when we start discussing percentiles.)

Let's Check Your Understanding

1. Kurtosis is _____.

2. When a curve is bell shaped and symmetrical but all scores cluster tightly around one central point, the curve is _____.

3. When a curve is bell shaped and symmetrical but all scores are spread out across the score range, the curve is _____.

4. When a curve is perfectly bell shaped and symmetrical, the curve is

   _____.

Our Model Answers

1. Kurtosis is **one aspect of how scores are distributed.**

2. When a curve is bell shaped and symmetrical but all scores cluster tightly around one central point, the curve is **leptokurtic.**

3. When a curve is bell shaped and symmetrical but all scores are spread out across the score range, the curve is **platykurtic.**

4. When a curve is perfectly bell shaped and symmetrical, the curve is **mesokurtic.**

Skewness

When one side of a curve is longer than the other, we have a *skewed distribution* (see Figure 3.2). What this really means is that a few people's scores

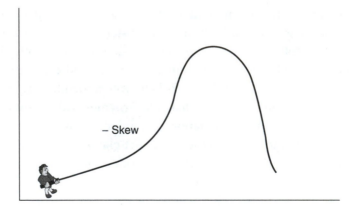

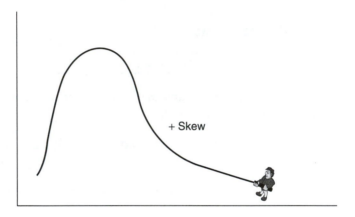

Figure 3.2   Skewness

did not fit neatly under the bell-shaped distribution and were either extremely high or extremely low. This makes one end of the curve longer than the other. The two ends of a curve are called its *tails*. All curves have two tails, whether they are long and flowing or stubby and cut off. On a symmetrical, normal curve, the two tails will fit on top of each other if you fold a drawing of the curve in half.

When a curve is skewed, one tail has run amok. When one or a few scores are much lower than all other scores, the tail is longer on the left side of the curve. This curve is called a *negatively skewed* curve. When one or a few scores are much higher than all other scores, the tail is longer on the right side of the curve. This curve is called a *positively skewed* curve. Since students often confuse what is negatively skewed and positively skewed, here's a memory hint: If the tail is long on the left, it's pointing to lower scores. On most tests, scoring low is not good—it's bad; it's negative! If the tail is long on the right, it is pointing to higher scores. Yea! Higher is usually better; this is positive! Those of us who tend to score in the average range, though, think of these high scorers as "curve wreckers." Figure 3.2 depicts both a negatively skewed curve and a positively skewed curve.

OK, let's see if we can make all of this more concrete by looking at the frequency distribution from Table 2.1. From this frequency distribution we can create our own frequency curve. To make this easier, here is Table 3.1 (previously shown as Table 2.1).

Just by eyeballing these scores, what conclusions can you draw? Hmmm. . . . Ask yourself, "Is there one score or a few scores clustered together that serve as a central point?" If you answered "No," good for you! Then ask yourself, "Are the scores spread out rather evenly (like melted butter)?" If you answered "Yes" this time, you are right again!!! So far, so good! Now, based on the fact that there's no real central point and the scores are spread out across the distribution, you wisely conclude that the curve is platykurtic.

Next, you need to determine if there might be distortions in the potential curve based on this frequency distribution. Ask yourself, "Are there any

Table 3.1   Frequency Distribution of Midterm Grades

Score X	f	Score X	f
100	1	77	
99		76	
98	1	75	1
97		74	
96		73	1
95	1	72	
94		71	1
93	2	70	
92		69	
91		68	
90	2	67	
89	1	66	
88		65	
87	2	64	
86	1	63	
85	3	62	
84		61	
83	1	60	
82		59	
81	2	58	
80	2	57	
79	1	56	1
78	1		

$$N = 25$$

extreme scores that are much higher or lower than the rest of the scores?" The correct answer is . . . Yes! One person scored really low with a score of only 56. The tail of this curve is pulled to the left and is pointing to this low score. This means that the curve is skewed in the negative direction.

Just by looking at this frequency distribution, you can conclude that the students were very spread out in their midterm grades and one person scored very differently (much worse) than the rest of the class. You should arrive at these same conclusions if you examine the grouped frequency distribution of the same test scores in Table 2.3 on page 23. All of the scores but one are somewhat evenly distributed across the intervals from 71–73 to 98–100. That one score in the 56–58 interval causes this platykurtic distribution to be negatively skewed.

Although eyeballing is a quick and dirty way of looking at your scores, a more accurate way is to graph the actual scores. As we told you at the beginning of this chapter, on the horizontal axis, typically called the *x-axis,* you list the possible scores in ascending order. If you are working with grouped frequency data, you list the intervals (see Figure 3.3). When you create a graph, however, let the midpoint of the interval represent the entire interval. On the vertical axis, typically called the *y-axis,* you list the frequencies in ascending order that represent the number of people who might have earned a score in each interval.

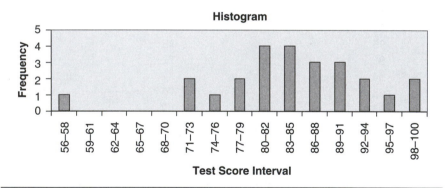

Figure 3.3   Graph of Grouped Midterm Scores

 Let's Check Your Understanding

1. What are the ends of a curve called?

_____

_____

2. What causes a curve to be skewed?

_____

_____

3. When a curve is negatively skewed, what conclusion can you make about how people scored?

_____

_____

 Our Model Answers

1. What are the ends of a curve called?
   The ends of a curve are called its *tails*.

2. What causes a curve to be skewed?
   When one or a few scores are much higher or lower than all other scores, the curve is skewed.

3. When a curve is negatively skewed, what conclusion can you make about how people scored?
   We can conclude that one or a few people scored much lower than all the other people.

Some Final Thoughts About Distribution of Test Scores

Creating a frequency curve of your scores allows you to see how scores are distributed across the score range. You can see the shape of the distribution and tell whether it is skewed. It is possible to create a frequency distribution from single scores and from grouped scores.

Key Terms

Let's see how well you understand the concepts we've presented in this chapter. Test your understanding by explaining the following concepts. If you are not sure, look back and reread.

- Frequency curve
- Kurtosis
  - Mesokurtic
  - Leptokurtic
  - Platykurtic

- Skewness
  - Positively skewed
  - Negatively skewed
- Graphs
  - *x*-axis
  - *y*-axis

Models and Self-instructional Exercises

Our Model

We have created a frequency curve by graphing the College Stress Scale test scores originally presented in the tables on pages 29 and 31.

f														
8														
7														
6								80						
5							74	80						
4					65	69	73	80	85					
3			54	60	64	69	73	79	84					
2	39	49	53	58	62	68	72	78	83	88	93			
1	36	46	52	56	62	67	71	77	81	86	92	99	104	110

36–40 41–45 46–50 51–55 56–60 61–65 66–70 71–75 76–80 81–85 86–90 91–95 96–100 101–105 106–110

Class Intervals for Scores

1. What does the *y*-axis represent?

   _____

   _____

2. What does the *x*-axis represent?

   _____

   _____

3. What is the kurtosis of this frequency curve?

   _____

   _____

4. Is this frequency curve skewed?

   _____

   _____

Our Model Answers

1. What does the *y*-axis represent?

   The frequency of people who could have gotten scores within each of the intervals appears next to the vertical axis. For our example, we used frequencies ranging from 0 to 8.

2. What does the *x*-axis represent?

   On the horizontal axis, we listed all of the possible class intervals.

3. What is the kurtosis of this frequency curve?

   Although not perfectly symmetrical, this distribution could be considered a normal, bell-shaped, mesokurtic curve.

4. Is this frequency curve skewed?

   It is not skewed because no scores are extremely larger or extremely smaller than all of the other scores.

Now It's Your Turn

Now it's your turn to practice using what you have learned. Using the social support data for Ryan and 39 other freshmen presented in Chapter 2, create your own frequency curve in the graph we have started on page 44. To help you, here is the grouped frequency distribution.

Class Interval	f	cf
29–30	3	40
27–28	4	37
25–26	4	32
23–24	6	28
21–22	7	23
19–20	6	16
17–18	4	10
15–16	4	6
13–14	1	2
11–12	1	1
$N = 40$	$i = 2$	

Remember that 40 freshmen took the social support inventory, so you should have 40 separate scores in your graph.

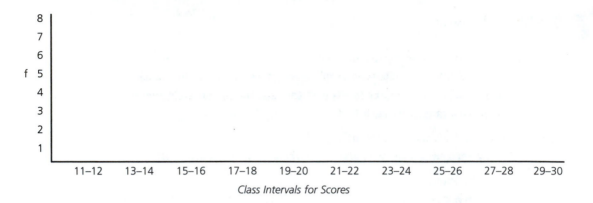

Class Intervals for Scores

Now that you've done this, you need to describe your frequency curve.

1. Is there one (or a few) score clustered together that serves as a central point?

_____

2. Are the scores spread out rather evenly (like melted butter) across the distribution?

_____

3. Based on your answers to these two questions, what can you conclude about kurtosis?

_____

4. Are there any extreme scores that are much higher or lower than the rest of the scores?

_____

5. Based on your answers to these questions, describe your frequency curve and what it tells you about how students scored on the social support inventory.

_____

_____

_____

_____

_____

Our Model Answers

f	11–12	13–14	15–16	17–18	19–20	21–22	23–24	25–26	27–28	29–30
8										
7						22				
6					20	22	24			
5					20	22	24			
4			16	18	20	21	24	26	28	
3			16	18	20	21	24	25	27	30
2			15	18	20	21	23	25	27	29
1	11	13	15	17	19	21	23	25	27	29

Class Intervals for Scores

1. Is there one (or a few) score clustered together that serve as a central point?

    Yes, scores are clustered around the interval 21–22.

2. Are the scores spread out rather evenly (like melted butter) across the distribution?

    No, they resemble a bell-shaped curve.

3. Based on your answers to these two questions, what can you conclude about kurtosis?

    The distribution is mesokurtic and is roughly symmetrical.

4. Are there any extreme scores that are much higher or lower than the rest of the scores?

    No, there are no extreme scores. This means that the curve is not skewed.

5. Based on your answers to these questions, describe your frequency curve and what it tells you about how students scored on the social support inventory.

    Scores on the social support inventory for this group of freshmen fell into a mesokurtic, bell-shaped curve. In addition, approximately half of them (19 students) scored between 19 and 24 on the inventory. No one had a really low score that was different from the rest of the group. Similarly, no one got a really high score. Forty points was the highest possible score on this 20-item inventory. (If you forgot the possible score range for this inventory, reread this section of Chapter 2.) We can conclude that Ryan and the other freshmen's scores are normally distributed in a mesokurtic, bell-shaped curve.

Words of Encouragement

It's time for us to say thank you for hanging in there. We are really concerned about helping you become knowledgeable about measurement, and you have been following our lead quite nicely. From what we can tell, you are just where you should be. Good work!! ☺

CHAPTER 4

Central Tendencies and Dispersion—Coming Together or Growing Apart

By now you might be thinking that we are pretty superficial people. In Chapter 3, we defined the "perfect body" simply by the shape of the frequency curve—its external appearance. If the curve was a person and we said it was beautiful because of its shape, you'd be right in calling us superficial. Since we definitely are not superficial, we want to extol some of the internal qualities that make the normal curve beautiful.

In measurement, internal qualities are reflected by the data that created the curve, by the statistics resulting from mathematically manipulating the data, and by the inferences that we can draw from these statistics. When we discussed scores, we were discussing data. Now it's time to move on to introduce you to some simple statistics related to the normal curve and measurement. On center stage we have that world-famous trio, The Central Tendencies.

Central Tendencies—The Inner Core of the Normal Curve

Before we introduce you to each member of the trio, we need to introduce the concept of central tendency. As Kranzler and Moursund (1999) state, "*central tendency* is a fancy statistical term that means, roughly, 'middleness'" (p. 7). When we talk about scores clustering together in the middle of a frequency curve, we are referring to the central tendency or the middleness of the curve. There are three measures of central tendency that you, as measurement specialists in training, need to become intimately familiar with: *mode, median,* and *mean* (see Figure 4.1).

Snapshots

© 2005 by Sharon E. Robinson Kurpius, Mary E. Stafford, and Jason Love

Figure 4.1 Central Tendencies

The Mode

The first of these, the *mode,* is a rather simple, straightforward character. Of all the central tendencies, the mode is the most instantly recognizable. When you look at a frequency curve, the score (or scores) obtained by the largest number of people is the mode. Let's consider the following set of scores (data) as a way to introduce mode:

1, 5, 9, 9, 9, 15, 20, 31, 32, 32, 32, 32

What is the mode? The answer is 32, because it occurs four times and no other score was earned as often.

In our example, let's change the score of 5 to a 9. Now, four people scored a 9 and four scored 32. This distribution is *bimodal* because it has two scores that have an equal highest frequency. Bimodal curves can still be symmetrical—even though this one isn't. Bimodal curves tend to look like a two-hump camel.

Now let's work with the data sets for midterm grades from Chapter 2. If you look at Table 2.1 on page 20, the midterm test score obtained by the largest number of students (in this case three students) is 85. Therefore, the mode for these midterm scores is 85.

When the midterm scores are grouped, we look at the class interval rather than the individual scores. The class interval that contains the largest number of people becomes the mode. For example, look at Table 2.3 on page 23. Four students scored in the 80–82 interval, and four students scored in the 83–85 interval. Because two intervals contained the same highest number of students, the frequency curve of these data is *bimodal*. When the two class intervals are adjacent to each other, as in this instance, the accepted procedure is to average the two midpoints and to report it as the mode. For example, when we average 81, the midpoint of the 80–82 interval, with 84, the midpoint of the 83–85 interval, we would report 82.5 as the mode.

Can you figure out what the mode is for the ungraphed stress scores for Ryan and his peers that we introduced in Chapter 2? Here are the 40 scores.

110	88	81	78	72	67	60	52
104	86	80	77	71	65	58	49
99	85	80	74	69	64	56	46
93	84	80	73	69	62	54	39
92	83	79	73	68	62	53	36

Even though the data (scores) are not graphed, you can see that three students scored 80. No other score was obtained by more than two students. Based on your examination of the scores, you can accurately conclude that the mode is 80.

Let's Check Your Understanding

Look at the grouped frequency data for these stress scores on the next page.

1. What class interval has the highest frequency of obtained scores?

_____

2. What is that frequency?

_____

Class Interval	f	cf
106–110	1	40
101–105	1	39
96–100	1	38
91–95	2	37
86–90	2	35
81–85	4	33
76–80	6	29
71–75	5	23
66–70	4	18
61–65	4	14
56–60	3	10
51–55	3	7
46–50	2	4
41–45		2
36–40	2	2
$N = 40$		$i = 5$

 ## Our Model Answers

1. What class interval has the highest frequency of obtained scores?
   The class interval is 76–80.

2. What is that frequency?
   The corresponding frequency is 6.

The Median

Now let's meet the second member of the trio—the *median*. At times this character is in plain view and at times it hides and you have to look between numbers to find it. The median is the score or potential score in a distribution of scores that divides the distribution of scores exactly in half. It is like the median on a highway—half of the highway is on one side and half on the other. As a matter of fact this is a good analogy for remembering what a median is. The median is the exact middle point, where 50% of the scores are higher than it and 50% are lower.

In order to find the median, first you have to order the scores by their numerical value, either in ascending or descending order. We suggest using ascending, since that is how most data are presented in measurement. To find this score, divide the total number of scores by 2. For example, if you have 40 scores, you would divide 40 by 2 and find that 20 scores are above and 20 scores are below the median. In this case, the median would be a theoretical number between the 20th and 21st scores. In fact, it would be the numerical average of the values of the 20th and 21st scores. If you have 45 scores, the median would be the 23rd score. When 45 is divided by 2, the median should be score 22.5 (rounded up to represent the actual 23rd score). We know that 22 scores will be below and 22 scores will be above the 23rd score.

When identifying the median, as well as the mode, the actual values of the scores aren't really important. You are just trying to find the middle score after ordering scores by their numerical value.

Let's play with a set of scores.

$$2, 6, 6, 7, 8, 9, 9, 9, 10$$

For this set of scores, the median score is 8, because four scores (2, 6, 6, 7) are below the score of 8 and four scores (9, 9, 9, 10) are above the score of 8. Finding the median is easiest when you have an odd number of scores. In this example, there are nine scores. The median has to be the fifth score, which divides the distribution evenly with four scores above and four scores below. (Just so you don't forget, the mode would be 9, since three people obtained a 9.)

OK, let's do another example. You are working with seven kids and give them a short spelling test. Their scores are 2, 6, 6, 7, 9, 9, and 10. What is the median score for this bimodal distribution? (You recognized that this is bimodal, didn't you, since there were two 6s and two 9s?) . . . And the answer is 7! A score of 7 has 50% of the scores (in this case three scores) above it and below it. It's a piece of cake to find the median when there is an odd number of scores. Just look for the one that is exactly in the middle.

Now let's find the median for a larger data set where you have an even number of scores.

$$1, 5, 9, 9, 9, 15, 20, 31, 32, 32, 32, 32$$

The first step is to list the scores in numerical order from smallest to largest. Lucky you, we've already done this. Your next step is to find out how many scores should be above and below your "theoretical" median. We say theoretical because the actual median score needs to be calculated and does not exist as a score obtained by someone in a data set with an even number of scores. This is one of those cases where the median is hiding between two numbers. Remember, in order to calculate the median score, we counted the actual number of obtained scores and divided it by 2. In this example there are 12 scores. (Remember, we write this as $N = 12$.) When we divide 12 by 2, we get 6. Our "theoretical" median will have six scores above it and six scores below it. If you separate this numerically-ordered data set into two groups of six, the line would go between the obtained scores of 15 and 20. The median is the arithmetic average of these two scores. For this example, the average of 15 and 20 is 17.5. This is our median.

The mode for this data set is 32. Even though both the mode of 32 and the median of 17.5 are measures of central tendency for the same set of scores, as you can see these two can be very different depending on whether or not the curve is skewed. The mode is not the best measure of central tendency because it does not reflect the entire data set. The median is a better measure of central tendency in that it tells you the middle point of the distribution. When the median is significantly smaller than the mode, your distribution is probably negatively skewed.

Let's Check Your Understanding

You give another spelling test; however, a new student has transferred to your class, increasing your class size to eight students ($N = 8$). On this spelling test, they scored:

$$4, 6, 6, 7, 7, 9, 9, 10$$

1. Where would you draw the line to divide this group exactly in half?

   Between _____ and _____.

2. What is the median score?

   _____

Our Model Answers

1. Where would you draw the line to divide this group exactly in half?
   Between 7 and 7. Good for you! You weren't tricked—the line goes between the two sevens. The actual numerical value of 7 is not important when you are dividing the scores into two groups, each of which contains 50% of the scores.

2. What is the median score?

    > The median score is 7. Even though common sense would tell you it's 7, let's be cautious and calculate it mathematically: (7 + 7)/2 = 7. Your median is the "theoretical 7" that was not actually obtained by a student in your class. In other words, it is not the 7 obtained by student 4 or the 7 obtained by student 5, it is the theoretical 7 that the theoretical student 4.5 would have obtained if he or she existed.

Medians and Modes for Grouped Frequency Data

We follow the same process when we have grouped frequency data. Let's find the median for the grouped frequency data presented in Table 2.3 on page 23. Twenty-five students ($N = 25$) took this midterm. Which student would divide the scores into two equal groups of 50% each? If you said student 13 (or the 13th score), you are exactly right. There are 12 scores above and 12 scores below this median point held by the 13th student. Now we need to figure out what class interval contains this 13th score. To find this out, look at the *cumulative frequency column* in Table 2.4 on page 26 and determine which class interval has a cumulative frequency that contains the 13th score or person. The interval 83–85 contains scores from persons 11, 12, 13, and 14. So, guess what? Your median is class interval 83–85, because this is where the 13th score or student is.

The mode is the interval that has the highest frequency. Two class intervals have a frequency of 4 each: 80–82 and 83–85. This grouped frequency distribution could be described as bimodal.

The Mean

It's time to introduce the leader of the pack, the one with the real clout when you have interval or ratio data—the *mean*. Unlike the mode and the median, the *numerical values of the actual scores in a data set are essential* when dealing with the mean. The mean, symbolized by M, is a mathematically determined number. It is the mathematical average of all the scores in the data set.

Just in case you've forgotten how to calculate an average, here's a reminder. Add up all the scores (remember that "X" stands for score) and then divide this sum by the number of scores you added (N). For example, for the spelling test scores of 2, 6, 6, 7, 9, 9, and 10, the *sum* (which is represented by the symbol Σ) of these is 49. When 49 is divided by 7 (the number of scores), the result is 7. The mean score for this spelling test is 7.

This 7 can be used to describe the average score that this class of students obtained on their spelling test. If we know nothing else about any student in this class, we would guess that if he or she took this spelling test, he or she would score a 7, the class mean. Do you see why the mean is so important?! For those of you who like to see formulas, this is the formula for a mean:

$$M = \frac{\Sigma X}{N}$$

That was so much fun, let's do it again. . . . Well, we thought it was fun. Let's calculate the mean on the second spelling test that eight students took. Their scores were

$$4, 6, 6, 7, 7, 9, 9, 10$$

What is the sum of these scores (ΣX)? If you added correctly, you should have gotten 58. When you divide 58 by 8 (the N or the number of scores you added up), you get 7.25. This is the class mean for this spelling test. Remember that the accepted practice is to report two decimal points.

 ## Let's Check Your Understanding

Let's get this central tendency trio singing and see if they sing in tune or in disharmony. Use the following data set. Use the space on the right as your work area.

$$1, 3, 3, 5, 5, 5, 7, 7, 9$$

1. What is the mode?

   _____

2. What is the median?

   _____

3. What is the mean?

   _____

 ## Our Model Answers

1. What is the mode?

   The mode = 5. By carefully scrutinizing these nine numbers, you wisely concluded that 5 was the mode. It was the score that appeared most frequently.

2. What is the median?

   The median = 5. You counted nine scores in all and divided it by 2. The middle score would separate the scores so that four would be above it and four below it. You quickly point to the middle 5 and say, "You there, you 5, you're the median."

3. What is the mean?

   The mean = 5. Being a budding measurement genius, you added the nine scores and arrived at a sum of 45. Dividing the 45 by 9, you conclude that 5 is the numerical value of the mean.

The mean, median, and mode each equals 5. When the three central tendencies have the same value, as in this example, they are singing in harmony and singing the exact same note. Most times, however, they just can't get it together (see Figure 4.1).

Now It's Your Turn

Let's check your understanding of central tendency with a new data set that might not be so harmonious:

10, 8, 6, 0, 8, 3, 2, 2, 8, 0

1. What's your first step?

   _____

2. Which score is obtained by the largest number of people?

   _____

3. What is this score called?

   _____

4. What is the *N* for this data set?

   _____

5. Between what two scores do you need to draw a line?

   _____

6. What is the numerical value of the median?

   _____

7. What is the ΣX?

_____

8. Finally, what is the mean?

_____

9. How would you describe the curve based on these measures of central tendencies?

_____

_____

 Our Model Answers

1. What's your first step?
   Reorder the data in ascending order to read: 0, 0, 2, 2, 3, 6, 8, 8, 8, 10.

2. Which score is obtained by the largest number of people?
   The score of 8 was the most frequently obtained score.

3. What is this score called?
   The mode!

4. What is the N for this data set?
   The N=10.

5. Between what two scores do you need to draw a line?
   Between the fifth and sixth scores.

6. What is the numerical value of the median?
   The fifth score = 3 and the sixth score = 6. The median is (3 + 6)/2 = 4.5.

7. What is the ΣX?
   The sum is 47.

8. Finally, what is the mean?
   $M = \Sigma X / N = 47/10 = 4.7$.

9. How would you describe the curve based on these measures of central tendencies?
   These three central tendencies do not coincide—they are in disharmony. Although the median and the mean are very close numerically, the mode is much larger. If you were to create a frequency curve for these data, it would be negatively skewed.

Some Final Points About Central Tendency

While the calculations or determinations of the mean, median, and mode are purely mechanical, the choice of which to use as a measure of central tendency and the interpretations about central tendency require judicious thought. Some considerations include the following:

1. For small data sets, the mode is unstable. (It can easily change by the addition of one or two scores.)

2. The median is *not* affected by the numerical value of the scores above or below it.

3. The mean *is* affected by the numerical value of every score in the group.

4. The mean is the most stable and reliable measure of central tendency for large groups ($N \geq 30$).

5. When the distribution of the data is symmetrical, the mean and median are identical.

6. In markedly skewed distributions, the median is the best measure of central tendency.

7. When the mode is much larger than the median and the mean, the curve is negatively skewed. In contrast, when the mode is much smaller than the median and the mean, the curve is positively skewed. Figure 4.2 shows you where the mean, median, and mode fall on the horizontal line of our graph when our curves are skewed.

Dispersion—Not All Bodies Are the Same

Measures of central tendency tell us about the concentration or clustering of a group of scores. *Measures of dispersion* tell us about the variability or how scores spread out within a group. The spread of scores helps to determine its kurtosis. Remember from the last chapter that a leptokurtic curve has little variability among the majority of its scores. In contrast, that flat, platykurtic curve receives its shape due to the great variability among scores. And, of course, the mesokurtic curve is the perfect curve with the scores spread out just right (the "perfect" body).

Range

One of the simplest measures of dispersion is the *range*. The range is the scale distance between the largest and smallest scores. For example, if the largest score on a test is 112 and the smallest is 16, the range = 112 – 16 = 96. The

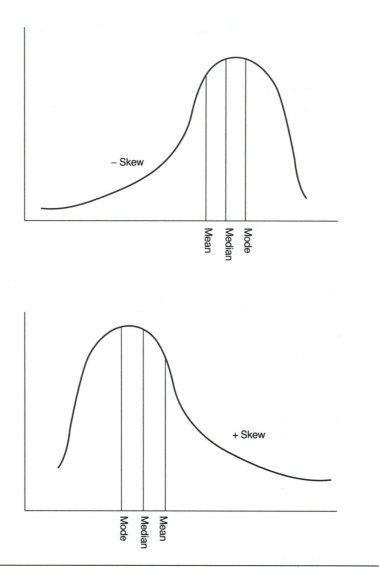

Figure 4.2   Mean, Median, and Mode on Skewed Curves

range for a set of scores where 93 is the highest score and 48 is the lowest would be what? Hmmm. . . . You're right; it is 45! $(93 - 48) = 45$. The range is a crude, simplistic measure of variability and is distorted by extreme scores. For example, if one person scored a 0 in the example we just did, the range would be 93; $93 - 0 = 93$. See how one person's score really distorts the range?!

Deviation Scores

Deviation scores also reflect the variation in a set of scores. A deviation score $(X - M)$ is the difference between any given score (X) and the group mean

(M). When you sum all of the deviation scores, the answer should always be 0. This is symbolized by

$$\Sigma(X - M) = 0$$

If you get any other answer than 0, check your math. You have (1) miscalculated the mean, (2) made a subtraction error when calculating the deviation scores, or (3) made a mistake in adding the deviation scores. It is also possible that if your mean was not an even number but included decimal points that you had to round off, the sum of your deviations around the mean will not be a perfect 0 but will be very, very close to it.

Variance

Calculating deviation scores is the first step in calculating variance. Since the sum of deviation scores equals 0, in order to use them to describe our curves, we square each deviation score before summing. We do this because it makes all of the deviation values positive and the sum becomes a number larger than 0. This process is symbolized by: $\Sigma(X - M)^2$, which is called the *sum of squares*. If the sum of squares (squared deviation scores) is divided by $N - 1$, the resulting measure of variability is the *variance* (denoted by s^2). Variance is an abstract construct that reflects a global variability in a set of scores. It becomes useful when we want to compare dispersion across different sets of scores. The formula for variance is

$$s^2 = \frac{\Sigma(X - M)^2}{N - 1}$$

We divide by $N - 1$ (remember N is our sample size). Subtracting 1 results in a denominator with a smaller value, which then results in a larger value for variance. This helps to control for the influence of sample size on variability.

Standard Deviation

Most of the time, however, we want to know dispersion within one set of scores. Some very wise mathematician figured out that the square root of variance is the *standard deviation,* a much more usable measure of dispersion. Standard deviation is symbolized by *s* or *SD*. The formula for *SD* is

$$SD = \sqrt{\frac{\Sigma(X - M)^2}{N - 1}}$$

The standard deviation is a very useful measure of variation or dispersion, because when we have a normal, bell-shaped curve we know what percent of the scores lie within one, two, or three standard deviations from the mean. Oh, the beauty of symmetry—the normal curve!! ☺

Between the mean (*M*) and one standard deviation (1*SD*) from the mean are 34.13% of all scores. Voila! If 1*SD* above the mean (+1*SD*) contains 34.13% of all scores and 1*SD* below the mean (−1*SD*) also contains 34.13% of the scores, we know that 1*SD* around the mean (±1*SD*) always, always, always contains 68.26% (34.13% +34.13%) of all the scores. You can see this in Figure 4.3. In measurement, if scores fall in the area between the mean and ±1*SD* from the mean, we consider these scores to be similar to each other. For tests in the social sciences (e.g., intelligence, personality, career tests), this is the area under the normal curve that is typically interpreted as "average."

On a normal curve, the area between 1*SD* and 2*SD* either above or below the mean always, always contains 13.59% of the scores. This is a fact, Jack!!

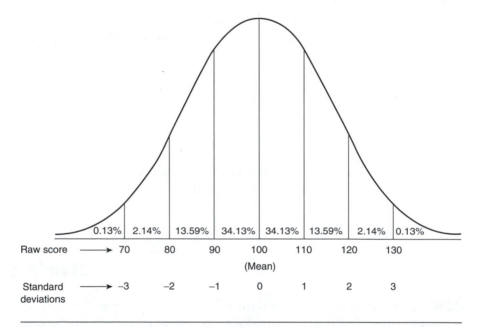

Figure 4.3   Normal Curve

Knowing this percentage is useful because we can add the 34.13% (the percentage of scores in the area 1SD from the mean) to the 13.59% (the percentage of scores in the area between 1SD and 2SD from the mean) and we will find that 47.72% of all scores can be found either 2SD above the mean or below it. Therefore, the $M \pm 2SD = 95.44\%$ (47.72% +47.72%) of all scores. Between the point 2SD below the mean and the point 2SD above the mean, 95.44% of all test scores can be found when we have a normal, bell-shaped curve.

If you were to score 2SD above or below the mean, you would be considered different from the average group on whatever construct was being measured. The more someone's score differs from the mean, the less they are like the majority of the people who took the same test. Measurement specialists start paying attention when someone's score is at least 2SD away from the mean.

Finally, it is also a fact that the area between 2SD and 3SD either above or below the mean contains 2.15% of all scores. If we add this 2.15% to the 47.72%, we get the percentage 49.87%. This 49.87% reflects the percentage of scores that fall between the mean and the point 3SD above it or that fall between the mean and 3SD below it. Therefore, the $M \pm 3SD = 99.74\%$ (49.87% + 49.87%) of all scores. When we have a normal, bell-shaped curve, almost all test scores can be found between the point 3SD below the mean and the point 3SD above the mean. Someone who scores at least 3SD away from the mean is very different from the majority of people who took the same test. How this person scored would be viewed as very different from how the average person would score on whatever construct is being measured. Measurement specialists love to study these people more closely.

Now you might have noticed that we failed to account for 0.26% of the scores (100% − 99.74% = 0.26%). This small percentage of scores reflects the most extreme scores that are found under the tails of our normal curve. In fact, if we divide 0.26% in half, we can say that 0.13% of the scores are greater than 3SD above the mean and are in the positive end of the curve and that 0.13% of the scores are less than 3SD below the mean and are in the negative end of the curve. This is depicted in Figure 4.3.

Before we challenge your understanding of measures of dispersion, we want to note two qualities of the SD. First, if there is no standard deviation (SD = 0), there is no dispersion. Everyone got exactly the same score. The curve is suffering from extreme "leptokurticism" and is no longer even a curve. Second, as the value of the SD gets larger, the scores are more spread out around the mean. There is greater variability among the scores and the curve becomes more platykurtic. When only one person gets each possible score, you get a flat horizontal line.

Let's Check Your Understanding

1. What is the range for a set of scores?

_____

_____

2. Since the sum of all deviation scores is _____, to use deviation scores to describe curves, we must _____ them.

3. Variance, symbolized by _____, is _____

_____.

4. The square root of variance is the _____.

5. On a normal curve, _____% of the scores falls either above or below the mean.

⭐ **Our Model Answers**

1. What is the range for a set of scores?
   The range is the scale distance between the largest and smallest scores.

2. Since the sum of all deviation scores is **0**, to use deviation scores to describe curves, we must **square** them.

3. Variance, symbolized by s^2, is **an abstract concept that reflects global variability in a set of scores.**

4. The square root of variance is the **standard deviation.**

5. On a normal curve, **50%** of the scores falls either above or below the mean.

Means and Standard Deviations in the Real World

Let's look at the mean and standard deviation for a quiz worth 35 points that your third period Algebra I class took. (Bet you didn't know you were an algebra teacher!) Their mean score was $17 (M = 17)$, and the standard deviation was $2 (SD = 2)$. Therefore, 68.26% of all the scores fall between 15 and 19 $(M \pm 1SD)$, 95.44% of all the scores fall between 13 and 21 $(M \pm 2SD)$, and 99.74% of all the scores fall between 11 and 23 $(M \pm 3SD)$.

Your fifth period Algebra I class also took the same quiz and their class mean was also $17 (M = 17)$, but their standard deviation was $5 (SD = 5)$. For this class, 68.26% of the quiz scores fall between 12 and 22 $(M \pm 1SD)$, 95.44% of the scores fall between 7 and 27 $(M \pm 2SD)$, and 99.74% of the scores fall between 2 and 32 $(M \pm 3SD)$.

By now you're probably saying to yourself, "Yeah, like I really care about this!" Well, you should. By knowing the mean score and the standard deviation for any test, you can make some basic comparisons among the individuals who took that test and across groups of people who take the same test. For example, although both algebra classes had a mean of $17 (M = 17)$ on the quiz, the standard deviations (SD) were not the same. The students in the third period class clustered more tightly around the mean of 17 in comparison to students in the fifth period class. We know this because of the sizes of the standard deviation for each class. There is greater variability in the quiz scores for the fifth period class $(SD = 5)$ than for the third period class $(SD = 2)$. We might conclude that those students in the third period class had a more similar understanding of the material on the algebra quiz (because they deviated less from the mean) than did the students in the fifth period class (who deviated more from the mean).

By squaring the standard deviations (SD^2), we get the variance (s^2) of each set of scores. For the third period class the variance is 4 $(s^2 = SD^2 = 2^2 = 4)$, and for the fifth period class the variance is 25 $(s^2 = SD^2 = 5^2 = 25)$. Just looking at these numbers, it is a good guess that these are unequal variances. There is a statistical procedure to test for equality of variances, but unfortunately (or fortunately, depending on your point of view) we aren't going to explore it. However, you should know that when two groups have very different variances on the same test, we have to be very, very careful about any conclusions we might make about their similarities or differences.

Recognizing the great differences in the two variances, as the algebra teacher, you should be wondering what is going on in the fifth period class that influenced such great variability in the students' scores. While measurement concepts in the abstract might be interesting to some of us, their application to the real world (such as these two classrooms) is why they're really important. Finding out what caused this variability will help you in bringing more students "up to par" on the algebra concepts you are trying to teach. This is truly what should be meant when we say "No child left behind!"

Key Terms

- Central tendency
  - Mean
  - Median
  - Mode
- Dispersion
  - Range
  - Deviation scores
  - Variance
  - Standard deviation

Models and Self-instructional Exercises

Our Model

Let's put all of this information about central tendency and dispersion together by examining a data set of only six scores. We've created a table with two columns that you'll need to complete in order to answer our questions.

X	$X - M$	$(X - M)^2$
3		
5		
5		
2		
6		
3		
$\Sigma X =$	$\Sigma(X - M) =$	$\Sigma(X - M)^2 =$

1. What is the mean?

   _____

2. What is the mode(s)?

   _____

3. What is the median?

   _____

4. What is the range?

   _____

5. What is the variance?

   _____

6. What is the standard deviation?

   _____

7. Between what two scores do 68.26% of the scores lie?

   Between _____ and _____.

8. Between what two scores do 95.44% of the scores lie?

   Between _____ and _____.

9. Between what two scores do 99.74% of the scores lie?

Between _____ and _____.

Our Model Answers

To help you see how we arrive at our model answers, we are going to talk you through our thought processes and then give you the answer.

1. What is the mean?

   Your first step will be to sum the X scores in the first column. Next you need to divide this sum by N to calculate the mean. What is your N? 6, because there are six scores.

   What is your M? $M = \dfrac{\Sigma X}{N} = \dfrac{24}{6} = 4.$

2. What is the mode(s)?

   This set of scores is bimodal with both 3 and 5 being modes.

3. What is the median?

   To find the median, we first need to reorder the scores in ascending order (2, 3, 3, 5, 5, 6). Since there are six scores, we know the median divides the scores so that three are above it and three are below it. The median is the average of the third score of 3 and the fourth score of 5. The median is $(3 + 5)/2 = 4$.

4. What is the range?

   The range is the difference between the highest score of 6 and the lowest score of 2. Range = $6 - 2 = 4$.

To help you find the rest of the answers, we have completed the values in the following table.

X	$X - M$	$(X - M)^2$
3	−1	1
5	1	1
5	1	1
2	−2	4
6	2	4
3	−1	1
$\Sigma X = 24$	$\Sigma(X - M) = 0$	$\Sigma(X - M)^2 = 12$

To get the deviation scores, we subtracted each individual score from the mean. We inserted the deviation scores into the second column. When we added these deviation scores, $\Sigma(X - M)$, we got 0. To complete the table, we squared each deviation score and inserted these values into the third column. The sum of the squared deviation scores, $\Sigma(X - M)^2$, equals 12.

5. What is the variance?

To calculate the variance you will use the formula

$$s^2 = \frac{\Sigma(X - M)^2}{N - 1}$$

So you need to know what $N - 1$ equals. $N - 1 = 5$.

$$s^2 = \frac{\Sigma(X - M)^2}{N - 1}$$

$$s^2 = \frac{12}{5} = 2.4$$

Answer: The variance is 2.4.

6. What is the standard deviation?

Remember that the standard deviation is the square root of the variance. A calculator would be helpful at this point.

$$SD = \sqrt{\frac{\Sigma(X - M)^2}{N - 1}} \quad \text{Or} \quad SD = \sqrt{s^2}$$

$$SD = \sqrt{2.4}$$

$$SD = 1.55$$

Answer: The standard deviation is 1.55.

7. Between what two scores do 68.26% of the scores lie?

To find these scores, you need to use the mean ($M = 4$) and standard deviation ($SD = 1.55$).

$$M + 1SD = 4 + 1.55 = 5.55$$
$$M - 1SD = 4 - 1.55 = 2.45$$

Answer: 68.26% of the scores lie between 2.45 and 5.55.

8. Between what two scores do 95.44% of the scores lie?

$$M + 2SD = 4 + 2(1.55) = 4 + 3.10 = 7.10$$
$$M - 2SD = 4 - 2(1.55) = 4 - 3.10 = 0.90$$

Answer: 95.44% of the scores lie between 0.90 and 7.10.

9. Between what two scores do 99.74% of the scores lie?

$$M + 3SD = 4 + 3(1.55) = 4 + 4.65 = 8.65$$
$$M - 3SD = 4 - 3(1.55) = 4 - 4.65 = -0.65$$

Answer: 99.74% of the scores lie between −0.65 and 8.65.

Now It's Your Turn

It is rare to have only six students take a test, such as in the example we just went through. So, let's work with the social support test scores we presented in Chapter 2. We want you to identify or calculate the measures of central tendency and the measures of dispersion for this set of data.

30	27	25	23	21	20	18	16
29	27	24	23	21	20	18	15
29	26	24	22	21	20	18	15
28	25	24	22	21	20	17	13
27	25	24	22	20	19	16	11

1. What is the mode?

   _____

2. What is the N?

   _____

3. What is the median?

   _____

4. What is the mean? (To make this easier for you, the sum of scores equals 866.)

   _____

5. What is the best measure of central tendency for these data and why?

   _____

   _____

6. What is the variance? (To make this easier for you, the sum of the squares of the deviation scores [$\Sigma(X - M)^2$] = 807.10.)

_____

_____

7. What is the standard deviation?

_____

8. Finally, between what sets of points do 68.26%, 95.44%, and 99.74% of the scores fall?

68.26%: Between _____ and _____.

95.44%: Between _____ and _____.

99.74%: Between _____ and _____.

9. As a measurement specialist in training, what conclusions might you make about Ryan, who scored 15 on this social support inventory; his best friend, Jason, who scored 11; his friend, Paula, who scored 26; and the student body president, Patricia, who scored 30?

_____

_____

_____

_____

 Our Model Answers

1. What is the mode?
   The mode is 20.

2. What is the N?
   $N = 40$.

3. What is the median?
   The median is between the 20th and 21st scores whose values just happen to be 20 and 21. So the median is 21.50.

4. What is the mean?
   The mean is 21.65. We got this by using the formula for the mean:

$$M = \frac{\Sigma X}{N} = \frac{866}{40} = 21.65$$

5. What is the best measure of central tendency for these data and why?

    The best measure of central tendency is the mean because this is a relatively large data set and the mean will be the most stable measure of central tendency. Furthermore, the three measures of central tendency tend to cluster together, so the mean is the best choice.

6. What is the variance?

    The variance is 20.695, which we would round up to 20.70. We got this by using the formula for the variance:

$$s^2 = \frac{\Sigma(X - M)^2}{N - 1} = \frac{807.10}{40 - 1} = \frac{807.10}{39} = 20.695$$

7. What is the standard deviation?

    The standard deviation is 4.55. We took the square root of 20.70 and got 4.55.

8. Finally, between what sets of points do 68.26%, 95.44%, and 99.74% of the scores fall?

    68.26% of the scores fall between 17.10 and 26.20.
    95.44% of the scores fall between 12.55 and 30.75.
    99.74% of the scores fall between 8.00 and 35.30.

9. As a measurement specialist in training, what conclusions might you make about Ryan, who scored 15 on this social support inventory; his best friend, Jason, who scored 11; his friend, Paula, who scored 26; and the student body president, Patricia, who scored 30?

    With a score of 15, Ryan is not similar to the majority of other freshmen and his score is more than 1SD below the mean. Jason reports even less social support than Ryan. Jason's score of 11 places him more than 2SD below the mean. In contrast, Paula scores right at the top of the area that is 1SD above the mean. Patricia reports even more social support with a score that is almost 2SD above the mean. Jason and Patricia have the most extreme scores for this group of students. Jason feels very unsupported socially and Patricia feels very socially supported. We should not ignore Ryan whose score was 1SD below the mean. He too feels unsupported socially.

Your New Best Friend—SPSS

Although we have walked you through this information using a paper-pencil approach, modern technology makes this process much, much easier. If this social support data set had been on a SPSS file, you could have clicked on Analyze and then on Descriptive Statistics. Under Descriptive

Statistics, click Frequencies and move the variable you want to examine to the Variables list by clicking on the arrow. Then click Statistics at the bottom of the Frequencies window. You will get another window that lets you check what measures of central tendency and what measures of dispersion you want calculated. If you would like to try this out, play with the data sets found on the Sage Web site: www.sagepub.com/kurpius.

 ## Words of Encouragement

We are so proud of you! We have had you tripping through a minefield of difficult measurement concepts and you have not fallen one time. (At least we didn't hear any explosions or see any body parts flying by us.) By mastering the material in this chapter, you are solidifying your understanding of frequency curves, particularly the normal, bell-shaped curve, and starting to use this understanding to make interpretations about test data. Way to go!!!!!

CHAPTER 5

Standardized Scores—Do You Measure Up?

So far, we've been working with what is called *raw data*. From this raw data or raw scores, we have been able to create frequency distributions and frequency curves and to examine measures of central tendency and of dispersion. These concepts are foundational to testing and measurement. It's time, however, to start learning more about scores themselves.

Often we want to compare people whom we assess with people who are more representative of others in general. Raw scores won't allow us to do this. With raw scores we can only compare the people within the same group who took the same test. We can't compare their scores to people who were not in the group that we tested. This is a dilemma! So what do we do?

Guess what?! You transform your raw scores to standard scores. When we standardize scores, we can compare scores for different groups of people and we can compare scores on different tests. This chapter will reveal the secrets of four different standard scores: *Percentiles, Z scores,* T *scores,* and *IQ scores.* Aren't you glad? (If you aren't glad now, you will be when you take your next exam.)

Percentiles—What They Mean in Measurement

Are you ready to begin? The first type of standard score is a percentile score. A *percentile* score, more commonly referred to as a *percentile rank,* represents the percentage of people in a group who scored at or below any given raw score. Crystal clear? Yeah, that sounds like gobbledygook to us too. So, maybe this example will make it clearer.

Let's start with a formula. Mathematically, a percentile rank (PR) equals the cumulative frequency (cf) that corresponds to a given (X) score (in this case, the one for which you are trying to find the percentile rank) divided by the number (N) of people in the frequency distribution and then multiplied by 100. The formula looks like this:

$$PR = \frac{cf}{N} \times 100$$

Figuring the PR is really simple and straightforward. So let's do it with the following data set:

X	f	cf
10	1	10
8	1	9
7	2	8
5	1	6
2	3	5
1	2	2

We want to know the percentile rank for a score of 2. Using the data above, what is the cf for a score of 2? THAT'S RIGHT—5. What is your sample size or N? RIGHT AGAIN—10. Good for you—you haven't forgotten how to read a cumulative frequency distribution. Now, let's plug these into our formula:

$$PR = \frac{cf}{N} \times 100$$

$$PR = \frac{5}{10} \times 100$$

$$PR = .5 \times 100$$

$$PR = 50$$

This PR of 50 means that 50% of the people who took this test scored 2 or below. (Gosh, they didn't do very well.)

Let's find the PR for the score of 8 using the same data set. The N has not changed. It is still 10. However, the cf has changed. It is now 9. When we plug this information into our formula, we get the following:

$$PR = \frac{cf}{N} \times 100$$

$$PR = \frac{9}{10} \times 100$$

$$PR = .9 \times 100$$

$$PR = 90$$

Anyone who scored an 8 on this test has a PR of 90 and scored the same as or better than 90% of the people who took this test. Pretty good, wouldn't you say?!

There are two things that we really want to make sure you understand.

Thing One: A percentile rank is not the same as a percentage, although they are closely related. The percentile rank tells us the rank of a score with respect to the group that the score is in. When you put a percentage sign with your percentile rank, you know the percentage of people who score at or below a raw score that corresponds to that percentile rank.

Thing Two: We talk about "scoring the same as or better than" a certain percentage of people who took the test. We do not say just "better than." (Some authors use the latter, but in measurement it's more accurate to think about a percentile rank as reflecting scores that are "the same as or better than.")

Percentile Ranks for Grouped Data

Although a similar process is used to calculate percentile rank for grouped data, more steps are involved. Don't let the formula scare you. We'll lead you through it bit by bit. It is very important for you to understand that when you have grouped (or interval) data, you are trying to determine the proportion of distance you will need to go into an interval in order to find the PR of a score that falls in the interval. To do this, these are the variables you need to be able to identify:

- X = raw score
- N = total number of people in the group
- i = interval width
- f_x = number of people with scores in the interval containing X
- cf_b = cf of the interval below the interval containing X
- LL = lower limit of the interval containing X (Remember LL from Chapter 2.)

The formula is

$$PR = \frac{[cf_b + f_x(\frac{X - LL}{i}) \times 100]}{N}$$

The formula may look overwhelming, but if you take it slowly and work from inside the first parentheses out, it's a piece of cake. The trick is doing it in little steps. Are you thinking, "OK, if you think it's so easy, you do it!"? OK, we will.

Here is a new set of grouped data. For this data set, what is the *PR* for a score of 21?

Interval	f	cf
25–29	5	30
20–24	5	25
15–19	10	20
10–14	2	10
5–9	5	8
0–4	3	3

First, we need to define each component of the equation.

- $X = 21$
- $N = 30$
- $i = 5$

- $f_x = 5$
- $cf_b = 20$
- $LL = 19.5$

Now, let's plug these values into the equation for PR.

$$PR = \frac{[cf_b + f_x(\frac{X - LL}{i}) \times 100]}{N}$$

$$PR = \frac{[20 + 5(\frac{21 - 19.5}{5}) \times 100]}{30}$$

$$PR = \frac{[20 + 5(\frac{1.5}{5}) \times 100]}{30}$$

$$PR = \frac{[20 + 5(.3) \times 100]}{30}$$

$$PR = \frac{(20 + 1.5) \times 100}{30}$$

$$PR = \frac{(21.5) \times 100}{30}$$

$$PR = .7167 \times 100$$

$$PR = 71.67$$

The *PR* for a score of 21 for this set of data is 71.67. This means that anyone who scored 21 scored the same as or better than 71.67% of the people in this data set.

Let's Check Your Understanding

Why don't you try it now? What is the *PR* for a score of 14 and what does this mean?

1. Find the values for the following components of the equation:

   - $X =$
   - $N =$
   - $i =$

   - $f_x =$
   - $cf_b =$
   - $LL =$

2. Plug these values into the equation for *PR*.

$$PR = \frac{[cf_b + f_x(\frac{X - LL}{i}) \times 100]}{N}$$

$$PR =$$

$$PR =$$

$$PR =$$

$$PR =$$

$$PR =$$

$$PR =$$

Hint: *PR* = 32.67. If you didn't get this answer, check out what we did on the next page.

3. What does this *PR* tell you?

_____

_____

 Our Model Answers

1. The values for the components of the equation are:

   - $X = 14$
   - $N = 30$
   - $i = 5$

   - $f_x = 2$
   - $cf_b = 8$
   - $LL = 9.5$

2. The completed equation is

$$PR = \frac{[cf_b + f_x(\frac{X - LL}{i}) \times 100]}{N}$$

$$PR = \frac{[8 + 2(\frac{14 - 9.5}{5}) \times 100]}{30}$$

$$PR = \frac{[8 + 2(\frac{4.5}{5}) \times 100]}{30}$$

$$PR = \frac{[8 + 2(.9) \times 100]}{30}$$

$$PR = \frac{(8 + 1.8) \times 100}{30}$$

$$PR = \frac{(9.8) \times 100}{30}$$

$$PR = .3267 \times 100$$

$$PR = 32.67$$

3. What does this *PR* tell you?

A person who scores 14 has a PR of 32.67. This means he or she scored the same as or better than 32.67% of the people who took this test.

Some Final Thoughts About Percentile Ranks

Another neat thing about percentile ranks is that you can also figure out what percentage of people or scores fell between two scores. So, if we asked you what percentage of people scored between 14 and 21, you now know everything you need to know to answer. Just subtract the *PR* for the score of 14 ($PR_{14} = 32.67$) from the *PR* for the score of 21 ($PR_{21} = 71.67$). Voila! ($PR_{21} - PR_{14} = 71.67 - 32.67 = 39$, which means that 39% of the people scored between scores of 14 and 21.) You can even go one step further and tell us the exact number of people who make up this 39% by multiplying the 0.39 by the number of people (*N*) who took the test ($0.39 \times N = 0.39 \times 30 = 11.7$). Therefore, you could tell us that 11.7 people scored between 14 and 21. We know, there's no such thing as a 0.7 person, but this is the mathematical answer so we'll live with it.

The beauty of a percentile rank and its accompanying percentile value is that it allows you to make accurate comparisons about people who took the same test and to draw conclusions about any one person in that group. It's also very convenient that you can use simple or grouped data and still draw accurate conclusions.

Remember that a *standard score* is a transformed raw score. A percentile rank is just one type of a standard score. There are other types of standard scores that are very important in measurement.

Z Scores

The foundational standard score in measurement is the Z *score.* A Z score is based on the normal, bell-shaped curve and is formed from deviation scores. Remember deviation scores from the last chapter? A deviation score is the difference between any one score and the mean $(X - M)$. If this deviation score is divided by the standard deviation (SD) for that group of scores, we have transformed the raw score into a Z score. The formula for a Z score is

$$Z = \frac{X - M}{SD}$$

A Z *score* is the deviation of a score from the mean expressed in standard deviation units. The sum of the Z scores is always zero $(\Sigma Z = 0)$. The mean for a curve of Z scores is also always 0, and the SD is always 1. That means that the variance (s^2) also equals 1. The Z scores below the mean have a negative value and those above the mean have a positive value. Z scores range from -4.00 to $+4.00$. The convention is to present Z scores with two decimal places. There is also a wonderful, helpful Z score table that can be found in most statistics books. We placed a Z score table in Appendix A.

Why Transform a Raw Score to a Z Score?

The value of transforming a raw score to a Z score is twofold.

Value One: Any score can be expressed as a percentile rank by referring its Z score to the normal, bell-shaped curve (see Figure 5.1). As you do this, you need to remember that between the mean and $1SD$ you have 34.13% of all scores, between 1 and $2SD$ you have 13.58% of all scores, and between $2SD$ and $3SD$ you have 2.14% of all scores. This is true whether you're looking at the portion of the curve above the mean or below it.

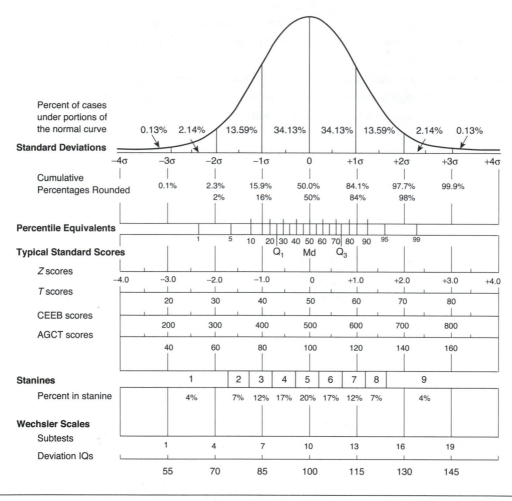

Figure 5.1   *Z* Scores and the Normal Curve

NOTE: This chart cannot be used to equate scores on one test to scores on another test. For example, both 600 on the CEEB and 120 on the AGCT are one standard deviation above their respective means, but they do not represent "equal" standings because the scores were obtained from different groups.

A *Z* of 0 is always located at the mean, which indicates that 50% of the scores fall below it and 50% of the scores fall above it. If someone's *Z* score is +1.00, it is 1*SD* above the mean. To calculate the percentile rank for a *Z* score of +1.00, we need to find the percentage of scores from the bottom point of the curve up to the *Z* score of +1.00. We do this by adding 34.13%, the percentage of scores between the mean and 1*SD* above the mean, to 50%, the percentage of all scores that fall below the mean.

$$+1Z = 34.13\% + 50\% = 84.13\%$$

We now know that the person who had a *Z* score of +1.00 scored the same as or better than 84.13% of the people who took this test. So this person's percentile rank is 84.13.

Now, if a person's Z score is -1.00, it is $1SD$ below the mean. To calculate the percentile rank for a Z score of -1.00, we need to find the percentage of scores from the bottom point of the curve up to the Z score of -1.00. We do this by subtracting 34.13%, the percentage of scores between $-1SD$ and the mean, from 50%, the percentage of scores that fall below the mean.

$$-1Z = 50\% - 34.13\% = 15.87\%$$

So, we know that the person who had a Z score of -1.00 scored the same as or better than 15.87% of the people who took this test. So this person's percentile rank is 15.87.

Value Two: The second value of transforming raw scores to Z scores is that we can compare one person's score on one test with his or her score on another test. Some people try to compare raw scores, but they are wrong, wrong, wrong! You can only make comparisons across tests when you have standardized both sets of test scores.

For example, you're the principal working at Martin Luther King Junior High School and you receive a phone call from the parents of one of your students, Simon. They are worried about the test papers he just brought home from his math and his English classes. His math test score was 48. His English test score was 58. His parents want to know if they should hire tutors to help Simon.

If you simply looked at his two raw scores, you might erroneously think he is doing better in English by his score of 58 than he is doing in math by his score of 48. This would be a mistake since these two tests have different means and standard deviations. Being the measurement scholar that you are, you know that you cannot compare raw scores, such as the ones Simon's parents gave you. Wisely, you consult his math and his English teachers to find out the class means and standard deviations on each of these tests. (Lucky you, these teachers were conscientious and had calculated these statistics.) The class math test mean was 40 and the SD was 8. The class English mean was 62 and the SD was 4. Because you know you can't compare raw scores, you standardize Simon's two test scores by using the handy-dandy Z score formula.

Simon's math test: $X = 48$	Simon's English test: $X = 58$
Class $M = 40$	Class $M = 62$
$SD = 8$	$SD = 4$
$Z = \dfrac{(X - M)}{SD}$	$Z = \dfrac{(X - M)}{SD}$
$Z = (48 - 40)/8$	$Z = (58 - 62)/4$
$Z = 1.00$	$Z = -1.00$

Even though Simon's raw score in English is higher than his raw score in math, you can tell that Simon did much better on his math test than on his English test just by eyeballing the standardized Z scores. Simon scored at the 84.13th percentile in math compared to his classmates. His percentile rank equals the percent of those who scored below the mean (50%) plus the percent of those who scored from the mean to $+1Z$ above the mean (PR_{+1Z} = 50% + 34.13% = 84.13%) or 84.13th percentile. However, he scored only at the 15.87th percentile in English (PR_{-1Z} = 50% −34.13% = 57.87%). Simon needs help in English. On this test he did better than only 15.87% of his classmates. You suggest to his parents that they should talk to his seventh-grade English teacher and maybe hire a tutor for English. Being a good principal, you also reassure Simon's parents that he seems to be doing well in math.

Let's do one more example. Remember our good friend Ryan who had complained about being stressed and not having any friends. He had taken both the College Stress Scale (CSS) and the Social Support Inventory (SSI). On the CSS, Ryan had scored 92. The mean for college freshmen was 71.78 with a SD of 16.76. On the SSI, Ryan had scored 15. The mean for college freshmen was 21.65 with a SD of 4.55. As Ryan's counselor, you are trying to decide whether to first address his loneliness or his stress. To help you make this decision, you want to compare Ryan's level of stress with his level of loneliness. To do this you have to transform his raw scores to Z scores.

Ryan's CSS score: $X = 92$	Ryan's SSI score: $X = 15$
Freshmen $M = 71.78$	Freshmen $M = 21.65$
$SD = 16.76$	$SD = 4.55$
$Z = \dfrac{(X - M)}{SD}$	$Z = \dfrac{(X - M)}{SD}$
$Z = (92 - 71.78)/16.76$	$Z = (15 - 21.65)/4.55$
$Z = +1.21$	$Z = -1.46$

If you were Ryan's counselor, you might conclude that he is both stressed (with a Z more than $1SD$ above the mean) and has little social support (with a Z almost $1.5SD$ below the mean). Clearly, he needs to learn how to make friends to build his support network. He could also benefit from some stress management training. You decide to focus on making friends while giving him some stress management techniques.

Let's Check Your Understanding

One of Ryan's two friends, Paula, also took the CSS and the SSI. What are the *Z* scores for each of Paula's test scores and how would you interpret them?

Paula's CSS score: $X = 75$	Paula's SSI score: $X = 26$
Freshmen $M = 71.78$	Freshmen $M = 21.65$
$SD = 16.76$	$SD = 4.55$
$Z = \dfrac{(X - M)}{SD}$	$Z = \dfrac{(X - M)}{SD}$
$Z =$	$Z =$
$Z =$	$Z =$

1. What does Paula's stress *Z* score tell us about her level of stress?

   _____

   _____

2. What does Paula's social support *Z* score tell us about her level of support?

   _____

   _____

3. Compare Paula's level of stress and social support.

   _____

   _____

4. Why would looking at her raw scores mislead you?

   _____

   _____

Our Model Answers

We've completed the table with the correct *Z* scores. How did you do?

Paula's CSS score: $X = 75$	Paula's SSI score: $X = 26$
Freshmen $M = 71.78$	Freshmen $M = 21.65$
$SD = 16.76$	$SD = 4.55$
$Z = \dfrac{(X - M)}{SD}$	$Z = \dfrac{(X - M)}{SD}$
$Z = \dfrac{(75 - 71.78)}{16.76}$	$Z = \dfrac{(26 - 21.65)}{4.55}$
$Z = +0.19$	$Z = +0.96$

1. What does Paula's stress Z score tell us about her level of stress?

   Paula's Z score is only +0.19, which is very close to the Z mean of 0. Paula seems to be perfectly average in her level of stress compared to other freshmen.

2. What does Paula's social support Z score tell us about her level of support?

   Paula's Z score is almost 1SD above the freshmen mean for social support. We can conclude that she has high average social support.

3. Compare Paula's level of stress and social support.

   Paula's Z scores fall within 1SD above the mean. This means that she is like most other freshmen (at least 68.26% of them). If we were to be very picky, we would also be able to conclude that she is almost above average in perceived social support and just about perfectly average in her experienced stress.

4. Why would looking at her raw scores mislead you?

   If we just looked at her score of 75 for stress and her score of 26 for social support, we might have concluded that she has more stress than support. How wrong we would be!!!

You are doing such a good job that we've decided to introduce you to the Z table that we've placed in Appendix A. Some brilliant mathematician (we don't know his or her name) calculated the exact percentile score to correspond with every possible Z value. For example, Ryan's Z score of +1.21 on the CSS means that he scored the same or higher than 88.69% of other freshmen on stress. We arrived at this value by looking at the Z value of +1.21 in the Z table in Appendix A and saw that this value reflected 38.69% of the area between the mean and 1.21SD above the mean. Because we wanted the percentile score, we could not ignore the 50% who scored below the Z mean of 0. When we added this 50% to the 38.69%, we know that Ryan scored at the 88.69th percentile.

For his social support Z score of −1.46, he scored the same as or higher than only 7.21% of other freshmen. We arrived at this value by looking at the Z value of −1.46 in the Z table in Appendix A and saw that this value represented 7.21% of the area below the Z score of −1.46. Therefore, we know that Ryan scored at the 7.21 percentile.

Now It's Your Turn

It's time for you to find the exact percentile ranks for Paula. Remember that her Z scores were +0.19 on the CSS and +0.96 on the SSI. OK, what are her percentile ranks?

1. CSS Z of +0.19 =

   _____

2. SSI Z of +0.96 =

   _____

(Hint: Don't forget to add the 50% who scored below the mean.)

Our Model Answers

1. CSS Z of +0.19 =
   The percentile rank for a Z score of +0.19 equals 57.53. We arrived at this value by looking at the Z value of +0.19 in Appendix A and found that this value represents 7.53% of the area between the mean and Z score. Because the Z value is positive, we have to add the 50% that represents the scores below the mean to the 7.53% and arrive at 57.53% of scores at or below a Z score of +0.19. Therefore, the percentile rank is 57.53.

2. SSI Z of +0.96 =
   The percentile rank for a Z score of +0.96 equals 83.15. We arrived at this value by looking at the Z value of +0.96 in Appendix A and found that this value represents 33.15% of the area between the mean and Z score. Because the Z value is positive, we again have to add the 50% that represents the scores below the mean to the 33.15% and arrive at 83.15% of scores at or below a Z score of +0.96. Therefore, the percentile rank is 83.15.

Other Standard Scores

Two other types of standard scores frequently used in measurement are T *scores* and *IQ scores*. Some of you may also be familiar with ACT, SAT, and

GRE scores, which are also standardized scores. For example, the GRE has a set mean of 500 and a *SD* of 100. Don't groan, your GRE Verbal of 490 wasn't that bad. You are rubbing elbows (literally and figuratively) with the average person who took the GRE.

T Scores

A frequently used standard score is the T *score*. *T* scores, often reported for personality inventories, have a mean of 50 and a standard deviation of 10. A *T* score is computed by multiplying the *Z* score by 10 and adding 50.

$$T = 10(Z) + 50$$

For Paula's stress *Z* score of +0.19, the equivalent *T* score is 51.9. We got this by doing the following:

$$T = 10(Z) + 50$$

$$T = 10(0.19) + 50$$

$$T = 1.9 + 50$$

$$T = 51.9$$

The *T* score becomes particularly useful when you are creating profiles of an individual. Two popular personality inventories, the *Personality Research Form* (PRF) and the *California Personality Inventory,* report results as *T* scores. Let's say on the PRF you score 40 (−1*SD* below the mean) and I score 60 (+1*SD* above the mean) on Dominance. My score is 2*SD* above yours. If I were you, I wouldn't get into an argument with me, because I have a much stronger need to dominate and win than you do. By knowing my *T* score, you know something about my personality and the strength of my personality characteristics in comparison to a norm group. (We will explain norm groups in Chapter 6.)

IQ Scores

A second frequently used standard score is the *IQ score*. Like *T* scores, IQ scores are derived from *Z* scores. (You probably didn't realize how valuable the *Z* score was going to be to your life.) The formula for converting a *Z* score to an IQ score is

$$IQ = SD(Z) + M$$

In this formula, you need to know the *SD* and *M* for the IQ test and the person's *Z* score.

Many intelligence tests use IQ scores that have a mean of 100 and a standard deviation of 15 or 16. For example, each of the Wechsler tests of intelligence has a mean of 100 and a *SD* of 15. The Binet IV has a mean of 100 and a *SD* of 16. For the Wechsler scales the formula for an IQ score is

$$IQ = 15(Z) + 100$$

The formula for an IQ score using the Binet IV would be

$$IQ = 16(Z) + 100$$

Most of the time you will not have to calculate a *T* score or an IQ score. Most assessment instruments will report results in standard scores or provide you with a table to convert raw scores directly to standard scores without having to calculate the *Z* score first. What you'll need to know, however, is how to compare and interpret these standard scores.

Let's look at an example. Simon's 15-year-old sister, Sarah, has been referred to the school psychologist for cutting classes. Sarah takes a series of tests including the Wechsler Intelligence Scale for Children, Fourth Edition (WISC-IV) and the PRF. Her IQ score on the WISC-IV is 133 and her *T* scores on the PRF are 39 for Harmavoidance, 62 for Play, 60 for Impulsivity, and 63 for Exhibitionism. Based on Sarah's IQ score of 133, it is evident that she is very bright. (Surely you saw that she was more than 2*SD* above the mean of 100.) Each of her scores on the PRF scales is one or more standard deviations away from the mean, which signifies that she tends to be extreme on these scales that happen to assess "at-risk" tendencies. She is a teenager who likes to have a good time (Play), doesn't think before she acts (Impulsivity), likes to be the center of attention among her friends (Exhibitionism), and is not careful in situations that could be harmful (Harmavoidance). Sarah needs to look at how these personality characteristics get her into trouble and how she can use her intelligence to help her make better decisions about her behaviors.

Key Terms

Check your understanding of the material by explaining the following concepts. If you aren't sure, look back and reread.

- Percentile rank
- *Z* score
- *T* score
- IQ score

Models and Self-instructional Exercises

Our Model

You may not know this, but when Gandalf (from *Lord of the Rings*) was selecting which Hobbits to help him fight the Dark Lord Sauron, he gave the Hobbits tests to measure courage, endurance, and power-hungriness. The Hobbits had a mean of 22 ($SD = 4$) on the courage scale, a mean of 53 ($SD = 7$) on the endurance scale, and a mean of 13 ($SD = 2$) on the power-hungriness scale. Mr. Frodo scored 30 on courage, 60 on endurance, and 7 on power-hungriness. Samwise Gamgee scored 26 on courage, 62 on endurance, and 9 on power-hungriness. Whom should Gandalf pick?

To answer this question, we first want to calculate the Z scores for both Mr. Frodo and Samwise on each scale.

	Mr. Frodo	Samwise Gamgee
Courage	$Z = \dfrac{X - M}{SD}$ $Z = \dfrac{30 - 22}{4}$ $Z = \dfrac{8}{4} = +2.00$	$Z = \dfrac{X - M}{SD}$ $Z = \dfrac{26 - 22}{4}$ $Z = \dfrac{4}{4} = +1.00$
Endurance	$Z = \dfrac{X - M}{SD}$ $Z = \dfrac{60 - 53}{7}$ $Z = \dfrac{7}{7} = +1.00$	$Z = \dfrac{X - M}{SD}$ $Z = \dfrac{62 - 53}{7}$ $Z = \dfrac{9}{7} = +1.29$
Power-hungriness	$Z = \dfrac{X - M}{SD}$ $Z = \dfrac{7 - 13}{2}$ $Z = \dfrac{-5}{2} = -2.50$	$Z = \dfrac{X - M}{SD}$ $Z = \dfrac{9 - 13}{2}$ $Z = \dfrac{-4}{2} = -2.00$

If we compare Mr. Frodo and Samwise Gamgee on their courage scores, Mr. Frodo, with a Z score of $+2.00$, is more courageous than 97.72% of the Hobbits who took this test. Although Sam, with a Z score of $+1.00$, is more courageous than 84.13% of the Hobbits who took this test, he is not as courageous as Mr. Frodo. Indeed, 13.59% of the Hobbits scored between

Mr. Frodo and Sam (97.72% − 84.13% = 13.59%). To get these figures, we remembered our normal curve and the percentage of people at different standard deviation points. If you need to refresh your memory, reread the beginning of this chapter.

Now let's compare our two courageous Hobbits on endurance. Mr. Frodo had a Z score of +1.00, which means he scored higher than 84.13% of the Hobbits. Sam had a Z score of +1.29, which means he scored higher than 90.15% of the Hobbits (we used the Z table in Appendix A to find this percentage). Samwise Gamgee has higher endurance than Mr. Frodo, even though they are both high in endurance. Approximately 6% of the Hobbits scored between Mr. Frodo and Sam (90.15% − 84.13% = 6.02%).

Finally, we need to look at their power-hungriness scores. Mr. Frodo had a Z score of −2.50. His need for power is higher than only 0.62% of the Hobbits. Sam had a Z score of −2.00, which means that his need for power is higher than 2.27% of the Hobbits. Neither Mr. Frodo nor Samwise has a drive to gain personal power.

When Gandalf looks at all of these Z scores and percentile ranks, he selects Mr. Frodo to be the ring bearer and the story's main character. However, Sam's extra high endurance coupled with his courage and low power-hungriness make him a perfect companion for Mr. Frodo as they try to destroy the ring and the Dark Lord Sauron.

Now It's Your Turn

Hey Dude!!! Do you remember Bill and Ted before they took their "excellent adventure"? They had just taken their midterms in history and political science. Bill, who hadn't been paying attention in either class, scored 58 in history and 65 in political science. Ted, who was no shining light, scored 55 in history and 68 in political science. Their class means were 78($SD = 10$) for history and 82($SD = 8$) for political science. Based on these data, complete the table on page 88 and answer questions 1 through 4. Hint: You will need to find the Z scores and use the Z table in Appendix A to help you find percentile ranks.

1. What was Bill's percentile rank in history and what percent of his classmates did he score better than?

   _____

2. What was Bill's percentile rank in political science and what percent of his classmates did he score better than?

   _____

3. What was Ted's percentile rank in history and what percent of his classmates did he score better than?

_____

4. What was Ted's percentile rank in political science and what percent of his classmates did he score better than?

_____

	Bill	Ted
History	$Z = \dfrac{X - M}{SD}$ $Z =$ $Z =$ $PR =$	$Z = \dfrac{X - M}{SD}$ $Z =$ $Z =$ $PR =$
Political Science	$Z = \dfrac{X - M}{SD}$ $Z =$ $Z =$ $PR =$	$Z = \dfrac{X - M}{SD}$ $Z =$ $Z =$ $PR =$

Their history teacher, Mr. Carlin, is trying to standardize the history scores so that students in different classes could be compared to each other. Mr. Carlin converts everyone's scores to T scores.

5. What is Bill's T score on his history exam?

_____

6. What is Ted's T score on his history exam?

_____

 Our Model Answers

To begin, we will first calculate the Z scores for both Bill and Ted for each class.

	Bill	Ted
History	$Z = \dfrac{X - M}{SD}$ $Z = \dfrac{58 - 78}{10}$ $Z = \dfrac{-20}{10} = -2.00$ PR = 2.27	$Z = \dfrac{X - M}{SD}$ $Z = \dfrac{55 - 78}{10}$ $Z = \dfrac{-23}{10} = -2.30$ PR = 1.07
Political Science	$Z = \dfrac{X - M}{SD}$ $Z = \dfrac{65 - 82}{8}$ $Z = \dfrac{-17}{8} = -2.13$ PR = 1.66	$Z = \dfrac{X - M}{SD}$ $Z = \dfrac{68 - 82}{8}$ $Z = \dfrac{-14}{8} = -1.75$ PR = 4.01

1. What was Bill's percentile rank in history and what percent of his classmates did he score better than?

    To find the percentile rank that corresponds with each Z score we looked at Appendix A. Because both of the Z scores for Bill were negative, we looked at the column that told us the area beyond the Z. We found that Bill's history Z score of −2.00 corresponds to a percentile rank of 2.27. Therefore, Bill scored better than 2.27% of the class in history.

2. What was Bill's percentile rank in political science and what percent of his classmates did he score better than?

    We looked for the corresponding percentile rank for Bill's political science Z score. His Z score of −2.13 corresponds to a percentile rank of 1.66, which means that Bill scored better than only 1.66% of the class in political science.

3. What was Ted's percentile rank in history and what percent of his classmates did he score better than?

    Ted's history Z score of −2.30 corresponds to a percentile rank of 1.07. Therefore, Ted scored better than only 1.07% of the history class.

4. What was Ted's percentile rank in political science and what percent of his classmates did he score better than?

    Finally, Ted's political science Z score of −1.75 corresponds to a percentile rank of 4.01, which means that he scored better than 4.01% of his political science classmates.

Bill and Ted are doing horribly in both history and political science. It is no wonder that George Carlin took them back in time to learn history from the people who are making it and to experience political science in the making. We surely hope that after their "excellent adventure," these Dudes would have scores higher than the class means.

When their history teacher computed the T scores, he used the formula that we gave you above:

$$T = 10(Z) + 50$$

5. What is Bill's T score on his history exam?

He converted Bill's history Z score into a T score in the following way:

$$T = 10 (-2.00) + 50$$
$$T = -20 + 50$$
$$T = 30$$

Bill's history T score is 30.

6. What is Ted's T score on his history exam?

Likewise, he converted Ted's history Z score into a T score in the following way:

$$T = 10(-2.30) + 50$$
$$T = -23 + 50$$
$$T = 27$$

Ted's history T score is 27.

Bill and Ted are certainly examples that not everyone is average.

Your New Best Friend—SPSS

If you know the mean and standard deviation for any data set, SPSS can quickly convert raw scores to standard scores. In the data-set window, you click Transform and then Compute. If you are converting to Z scores, under Target Variable you might want to label your new variable z (something). If you are converting to T scores, you might want to call it t (something). Under Numeric Expression, you will use the appropriate standardization formula we gave you above. Maybe an example will make this clearer.

Let's convert the midterm raw scores we introduced in Chapter 2 (Table 2.1, p. 20) to Z scores. The midterm data set can be found on the Sage Web site (www.sagepub.com/kurpius). In the SPSS program, click Transform and then Compute. In the new window, call your target variable *zmidterm*. Under Numeric Expression, put the formula "(midterm − 84)/9.41." The mean for the midterm grades was 84 and the standard deviation was 9.41. When you click OK, the computer will calculate a *zmidterm* score to match each raw midterm score. If you did this correctly, your *zmidterm* scores should be exactly the same as our *zmid* scores.

Words of Encouragement

Unlike Bill and Ted, you have the potential to be curve-wreckers with your newfound knowledge of standard scores. If you have diligently followed everything we have done step-by-step, you are able to calculate and interpret standard scores. Good job!!!

CHAPTER 6

Norms and Criterion Scores—Keeping Up With the Joneses or Not

H ere we go again—something new for you to learn. This is going to be a short and to the point chapter. Aren't you glad? We are going to introduce you formally to criterion-referenced tests and norm-referenced tests. Just to remind you, a *test* is a sample of behavior or characteristic at a given point in time.

Criterion-Referenced Tests—Do You Know as Much as You Should?

To keep this simple, first we need to define what a criterion is. In the context of measurement, a *criterion* is defined as some measurable behavior, knowledge, attitude, or proficiency. A *criterion-referenced test* is a mastery test that assesses your proficiency on a criterion of importance. For example, perhaps your professor at the beginning of the semester told you that you had to learn 70% of the information related to measurement in order to pass this class. You demonstrate that you've learned this information by averaging at least 70% across all the class tests and other assignments. In this instance, the criterion is the course content, and the *cutoff score* for passing is 70%. A cutoff score is the lowest score you can receive and still be in the passing range.

As we see increasing demands for accountability in education, both students and teachers are having to pass criterion-referenced tests on specific domains of knowledge. For example, in many states students must pass knowledge-based competency exams in order to receive their high school diploma. This is called *high-stakes* testing.

Teachers also have to demonstrate command of specific knowledge through state-administered criterion-referenced tests in order to become certified as teachers. Indeed, this is also true for almost anyone who is seeking any type of state certification (attorneys, physicians, nurses, psychologists, counselors, certified professional accountants, etc.). In fact, in many, many fields, people have to demonstrate on a test that they have mastered a certain body of knowledge in order to receive some type of degree or recognition. Each one of these tests is a criterion-referenced test.

Those who give criterion-referenced tests can set multiple cutoff scores. For example, on your course syllabus, your professor may say, "If you demonstrate that you know 90% of the course content on your exams, you will earn an A." Professors who do this typically award a B for 80%, C for 70%, and a D for 60%. This professor has established four different cutoff scores and equated grades to each one of the cutoffs.

See, we told you this would be straightforward, simple information! On the criterion-referenced test assessing this information, we bet you'll get at least a 90%.

 Let's Check Your Understanding

1. What is a criterion?

   _____

   _____

2. What is a criterion-referenced test?

   _____

   _____

3. What is a cutoff score?

   _____

   _____

 Our Model Answers

1. What is a criterion?

   A criterion is some measurable behavior, knowledge, attitude, or proficiency.

2. What is a criterion-referenced test?

   A criterion-referenced test is a mastery test that assesses your proficiency on a criterion of importance.

3. What is a cutoff score?

   A cutoff score is the lowest score you can receive and still be in the passing range.

Norm-Referenced Tests—Dying to Fit In

What a serious title—Dying to Fit In! Don't worry; we're not going to kill you with this information. A *norm-referenced test* is one in which scores are distributed into a bell-shaped curve and a person's performance, behavior, knowledge, or attitude score is interpreted with respect to the normal curve.

We've already talked about the normal curve. Remember the nice, perfect, bell-shaped curve? Well, the scores from people in *norm groups* are what created this bell-shaped curve. A *norm group* is made up of a large representative group of people who took the test and on whom the test was standardized. The importance of the norm group is that it shows what is the normal or average performance for groups of people. Therefore, defining who the "groups of people" are is critical. Measurement specialists primarily talk about three types of norm groups: the *normative sample, fixed-reference groups,* and *specific group norms*.

The Norm-Reference Group

Any norm group must reflect the population from which it is drawn. The test manual, therefore, must accurately describe the individuals who make up the norm group (also called the *norm-reference group* or the *normative sample*). For example, a nationally used achievement test for middle school students must establish a national norm with students from all grade levels of middle school. The normative sample must also be large enough to be reflective of middle school students in general. If we want to be very specific about a normative sample, we would ideally require that the sample includes

- Children from every region of the United States
- Children from rural, urban, and inner-city schools
- Both boys and girls
- Children representing all racial or ethnic groups
- Children from all socioeconomic status levels
- Children from all grade levels for which the test is appropriate

If the authors of this achievement test have drawn an adequate normative sample that includes sufficient numbers of children from all of the categories above, they can make an inference that the sample represents the larger population of middle school children in the United States. This inference is important. The normative sample makes up the bell-shaped, normal curve against which you compare an individual student's score. However, you want to generalize beyond the norm group to all children with similar characteristics. This generalization or inference is only possible if the children in the normative sample are representative of the larger population of children.

The size of the normative sample must be large enough so that you have stable values for the scores that make up the normal curve. To get a truly representative normative sample that represents the larger national population, test developers should establish a norm for their tests on thousands of people.

Let's put this into perspective by looking at Jesse's scores on his seventh-grade achievement test. It is April, and Jesse, along with everyone else in his middle school, has taken the Stanford Achievement Test. When Jesse and his family receive his results, they are reported as percentile scores. The norm group to which Jesse's raw scores were compared to get his percentile scores was a normative sample based on children across the United States. For the children in the normative sample, their raw scores had been standardized into percentile scores. (And of course you remember that the mean percentile score is 50.) If Jesse's math score was in the 35th percentile, we know that his knowledge of math is the same as or better than the knowledge of only 35% of seventh-grade children nationally. If his math score had been in the 85th percentile, we can conclude that Jesse's knowledge of math is the same as or better than that of 85% of seventh-grade children nationally.

Some cautions are in order.

1. Jesse must have similar demographic characteristics to the children in the norm group.

2. Jesse must have sufficient knowledge and use of the English language to make the test scores meaningful.

3. Jesse's scores can only be compared to the norm group made up of seventh graders—not sixth graders and not eighth graders.

The Fixed-Reference Group

A *fixed-reference group* can be a subgroup of the norm-reference group. Often, you will find norm tables for subgroups in a test manual. If Jesse was a Latino student and the manual broke the larger norm-reference group into fixed-reference groups based on race or ethnicity, you could compare Jesse's scores to those of other Latino seventh-grade students. Almost all test manuals will provide you with fixed-reference group norms based on gender. Many also will provide you with norms for public versus private schools and for clinical versus "normal" samples. If you are making a decision about a student's placement in school, it is essential that you compare his or her scores to as many relevant and appropriate fixed-reference groups as possible.

Let's look at Jesse's math score again. The manual doesn't report fixed-reference groups based on race or ethnicity, but it does provide gender-based fixed-reference norms. Jesse is a boy, so you look at the norm table for boys and find that his score places him in the 65th percentile compared to similar boys nationally. Just because you're curious, you look at the norm table for girls. Jesse's score places him in the 70th percentile among girls. See, gender is important, so don't ignore it!

Specific Group Norms

Specific group norms become relevant when you standardize a test on a narrowly defined population. State Departments of Education are notorious for developing specific or *local norms*. These might include norms for students statewide, for regions of the state, for specific school districts, and for individual schools. Although local norms can give very interesting information, the question remains whether the subgroups are sufficiently large to allow for meaningful comparisons. Perhaps the following example will clarify what is meant by specific or local norms and how they can be useful.

The principal of Jesse's school asked her State Department of Education for specific norms by grade for her school and norms for all other schools in her school district. This allows her and her teachers to compare individual students to their classmates in the same school and to compare them to students in other schools in the same school district. This might give teachers more insight into individual students. It can provide the principal with information about the performance of students in her school in comparison to students in all of the other schools in the same district.

Sadly, this information can also be misused to penalize teachers and schools whose students do not perform as well as students in other schools. Sometimes people forget that when scores become standardized they are forced into the normal, bell-shaped curve. By definition, 50% must be below the mean. Only in Lake Wobegon are all children above average! They refused to be part of a norm-reference group.

Let's Check Your Understanding

1. What is a norm-referenced test?

   _____

   _____

2. What is a norm group?

   _____

   _____

3. In an ideal world, manuals for norm-referenced tests would present norms for _____, _____, and _____.

4. Three types of norm groups are

   _____, _____,

   and/or _____.

 Our Model Answers

1. What is a norm-referenced test?
   A norm-referenced test is one in which scores are distributed into a bell-shaped curve and a person's performance, behavior, knowledge, or attitude score is interpreted with respect to the normal curve.

2. What is a norm group?
   A norm group is made up of a large representative group of people who took the test and on whom the test was standardized.

3. In an ideal world, manuals for norm-referenced tests would present norms for **gender, age or grade level, race or ethnicity, socioeconomic status, rural/urban/inner-city settings, and/or geographic region.**

4. Three types of norm groups are **normative sample, fixed-reference groups, and specific group or local norms.**

Key Terms

- Criterion-referenced tests
  - Criterion
  - Cutoff score
- Norm-referenced tests
- Norm groups
  - Norm-reference group
  - Fixed-reference group
  - Specific group norms

Models and Self-instructional Exercises

You have just taken your midterm in this class (again), and you find out you knew 60% of the information on the test. (Careful, you're slipping!)

1. Are you hoping this is a criterion-referenced or norm-referenced test?

   _____

   _____

2. Explain what your score could mean for your grade if the test is criterion-referenced.

   _____

   _____

   _____

3. Explain what your score could mean for your grade if the test is norm-referenced.

   _____

   _____

   _____

   _____

 ## Our Model Answers

You have just taken your midterm in this class (again), and you find out you knew 60% of the information on the test.

1. Are you hoping this is a criterion-referenced or norm-referenced test?

   If we had taken this test and got 60% of the answers correct, we would want the test to be norm-referenced.

2. Explain what your score could mean for your grade if the test is criterion-referenced.

   Your score indicates that you only learned 60% of the knowledge domain being tested. Most professors would probably give you a D at best on your midterm.

3. Explain what your score could mean for your grade if the test is norm-referenced.

If this test was norm-referenced, your score of 60% could still be a good score, depending on how everyone else in the class did. We can always hope that you scored better than most of your classmates and are on the upper end of the bell-shaped curve based on class scores.

Words of Encouragement

Do you realize that you have finished almost 60% of this book? As the commercial says, "You've come a long way, baby." If you keep hanging in with us, we'll help you have not only great scores on a norm-referenced test but also on criterion-referenced tests—at least for this measurement material.

CHAPTER 7

Error Scores—The Truth, the Whole Truth, and Nothing but the Truth?

Wouldn't it be wonderful if a test score was an absolutely perfect, accurate measure of whatever behavior or variable is being measured? Sadly, test scores are not all they're cracked up to be. They are not perfect measures of knowledge, behaviors, traits, or any specific characteristic. That's right, even the tests in this class are not perfect measures of what you know. Basic test theory can help us explain why test scores are fallible.

Test Theory

A basic concept in test theory is that any score obtained by an individual on a test is made up of two components: the *true score* and the *error score*. No person's obtained test score (X_o) is a perfect reflection of his or her abilities, or behaviors, or characteristics, or whatever it is that is being measured. The basic equation that reflects the relationship between true, error, and obtained or observed scores is

$$X_o = X_t + X_e$$

In this basic test theory equation, the variables are

- X_o = the score obtained by a person taking the exam (referred to as an *obtained score* or *observed score*)
- X_t = a person's true score
- X_e = the error score associated with the obtained score

As is evident in the equation, if there was no error ($X_e = 0$), the obtained score would also be the true score ($X_o = X_t + 0$, which is $X_o = X_t$). Unfortunately, we know of *no* situation that does not contain at least a bit of error or a person who is absolutely perfect. Even Mary Poppins was only "practically perfect."

This naturally leads to a need to explain sources of error in testing. While we would love to explain it, we can't. Error just happens, even though we do know of some factors related to error. There can be error that will increase your test score. On the other hand, there can also be error that will decrease your test score (we're making the assumption that a higher test score is better). Sources of error that might help increase scores can be things or conditions such as (1) getting a good night's sleep before the exam, (2) being able to remember everything you studied, (3) being a good guesser, (4) being emotionally calm, (5) being in a comfortable and quiet test environment, and (6) feeling good about your world. For example, research has shown that sitting at a table is more conducive to test taking than sitting at a desk with a folding arm. You will also do better on your exams if you've slept well the night before and have eaten healthy meals.

Some of the sources of error that might decrease scores include (1) being hungry or thirsty, (2) being physically tired, (3) not carefully reading the test questions, (4) being emotionally upset, (5) being in a noisy, poorly lit, and uncomfortable test environment, (6) responding carelessly, and (7) not feeling well. I bet you can remember a time you had to take a test and you had a head cold. It was hard to think, wasn't it? It's also hard to concentrate on taking a test if you are emotionally upset. If you've had an argument with your parents or with your boyfriend or girlfriend, you probably experienced emotional agitation that interfered with recall and concentration. Just think of a boy who comes to school and takes an achievement test when his parents have been in a drunken argument all night. Not only did he not get a good night's rest, but he is very worried about his parents. Certainly, his obtained achievement score will be affected by these sources of error (error score). Let's review with some basic questions.

 ## Let's Check Your Understanding

1. The basic test-theory equation is $X_o = X_t + X_e$. According to this equation, the obtained score is a mathematical combination of the _____ score and the _____ score.

2. This equation can also be rewritten as $X_t = X_o - X_e$. Explain the meaning of this equation.

_____

_____

3. An exact or perfect measure of a variable is a person's _____ score.

4. Good guessing is a source of _____.

Our Model Answers

1. The basic test theory equation is $X_o = X_t + X_e$. According to this equation, the obtained score is a mathematical combination of the **true** score and the **error** score.

2. This equation can also be rewritten as $X_t = X_o - X_e$. Explain the meaning of this equation.
   The true score is a combination of an observed score and an error score.

3. An exact or perfect measure of a variable is a person's **true** score.

4. Good guessing is a source of **error.**

Test-Theory Assumptions

There are three underlying assumptions in test theory. They are relatively simple and straightforward. First, it is assumed that true scores are stable and consistent measures of a variable, characteristic, behavior, or whatever you're measuring. Therefore, when you are doing measurement, you try to control for as much error as possible so that your observed score approaches your true score. We want our observed score to be as close as possible to our true score (which we will never really know).

The second assumption is that error scores are random. They just happen. As measurement specialists, we try to stamp out as much error as we can, but error can't be totally controlled. Every obtained score consists of error. Error doesn't care where it strikes. It attaches itself to every score, just like a leech, regardless of who is taking the test. Because error attaches itself to the true score, it can raise or lower an obtained score. Error scores occur purely by chance. Because of this, there is no (zip, nada, zilch) relationship between error scores and obtained scores (or true scores for that matter). What this means is that "a student with a high score on a test should be just as likely to have a large error associated with his [or her] score, either positive or negative, as the person who received the lowest score on the test" (Dick & Hagerty, 1971, p. 12).

The final assumption is that the observed score is the sum of the true score and the error score ($X_o = X_t + X_e$). In order to understand this assumption, we need to understand Thing One and Thing Two (if Dr. Seuss were writing this book) and we need an example. This "theoretical" example can be found in Table 7.1. We say theoretical because we can never know what someone's error score is.

Table 7.1   True, Error, and Observed Scores and Their Sums, Means, and Variances

Student	True score X_t	Error Score X_e	Obtained Score X_o
1	80	+2	82
2	91	−3	88
3	95	0	95
4	88	−1	87
5	85	+4	89
6	91	+3	94
7	80	−2	78
8	94	0	94
9	88	+1	89
10	85	−4	81
$\Sigma X =$	877	0	877
$M =$	87.7	0.0	87.7
$\sigma^2 =$	24.81	6.0	30.81
$\sigma =$	4.98	2.4	5.55

Thing One: The mean of error scores across individuals on a test always equals 0. In order for this to be true, some people have "positive" error and other people have "negative" error; thus, the amount of positive error added to the amount of negative error equals 0. If you don't believe us, look at Table 7.1 and add the values in the error score (X_e) column. As is blatantly obvious, if you add up the positive numbers (2, 4, 3, and 1), the total is 10. If you add up the negative numbers (−3, −1, −2, and −4), the total is −10. The positive number sum (10) added to the negative number sum (−10) equals 0.

Thing Two: Although the mean is 0, everyone does not have the same error score. Therefore, there is error variance. Just as error attaches itself to the true score to yield the obtained score, so does error variance (σ_e^2) attach itself to the variance of the true score (σ_t^2) to yield the variance of the obtained score (σ_o^2). Classic test theory depicts the relationship among these three types of variance by the following equation:

$$\sigma_o^2 = \sigma_t^2 + \sigma_e^2$$

Where

σ_o^2 = variance of the obtained (observed) scores

σ_t^2 = variance of the true scores

σ_e^2 = variance of the error scores

To see this relationship, add the true variance, σ_t^2 to the error variance σ_e^2 in Table 7.1. As you can see, when the σ_t^2 of 24.81 is added to the σ_e^2 of 6.0, this equals the σ_o^2 of 30.81.

Now that we've taught you this, we have to "fess up." We can't know the actual values of error scores or true scores, so we can't calculate their variances. They are hypothetical concepts. You just have to trust us that they exist. In fact, the error scores, because they are random, are totally independent of (that is, not correlated with) the true scores. So now you have some idea about the theoretical underpinnings of testing.

Let's Check Your Understanding

1. One assumption of test theory is that true scores reflect relatively _____ or _____ variables/characteristics/behaviors of the test taker.

2. Another assumption of test theory is that the error score you get is a matter of _____ or _____.

3. The sum of error scores across people on a test equals _____.

4. A person who scores high on a test has more positive error than a person who scores low. True or false?

5. If the person giving the test tries hard enough, he or she can control almost all of the error. True or false?

6. Write an equation that shows the relationship between obtained score variance, true score variance, and error variance.

   _____

7. If everyone in this class made the same grade on the midterm exam, why would you think there was something fishy about their scores? Explain why in terms of test theory.

_____

_____

_____

 ## Our Model Answers

1. One assumption of test theory is that true scores reflect relatively **stable** or **consistent** variables/characteristics/behaviors of the test taker.

2. Another assumption of test theory is that the error score you get is a matter of **chance** or **randomness.**

3. The sum of error scores across people on a test equals **0.**

4. A person who scores high on a test has more positive error than a person who scores low. True or false?
   False. Error is random and has no relationship with the obtained scores.

5. If the person giving the test tries hard enough, he or she can control almost all of the error. True or false?
   False. The fact that error is random means you have no control over it.

6. Write an equation that shows the relationship between obtained score variance, true score variance, and error variance.
   $$\sigma_o^2 = \sigma_t^2 + \sigma_e^2$$

7. If everyone in this class made the same grade on the midterm exam, why would you think there was something fishy about their scores? Explain why in terms of test theory.
   Because everyone has an individual error score and an individual true score, the probability that everyone would get the same test score is once again zilch, zip, nada, highly unlikely, a fluke of nature.

Key Terms

- True score
- Error score
- Obtained score
- Basic test-theory equation

Models and Self-instructional Exercises

Now that you have grasped the concepts of true scores, error scores, and obtained scores and completely understand traditional test theory (careful, you are in danger of becoming practically perfect like Mary Poppins), let's do a model exercise.

Our Model

Following are data for a small class of 10 students who took a 50-item true–false exam in their economics class. We have provided the sums, means, variances, and standard deviations for the true and error scores.

1. Calculate the obtained scores for each student.

2. Calculate the ΣX for each type of score.

3. Calculate the M for each type of score.

4. Calculate the σ^2 for each type of score.

5. Finally, check yourself to see whether the following equation is true for this set of data: $\sigma_o^2 = \sigma_t^2 + \sigma_e^2$.

Student	True score X_t	Error Score X_e	Obtained Score X_o
1	46	−2	
2	35	+4	
3	24	−6	
4	40	0	
5	24	+6	
6	35	−4	
7	28	−1	
8	28	+1	
9	46	+2	
10	41	0	
$\Sigma X =$			
$M =$			
$\sigma^2 =$			
$\sigma =$	8.01	3.38	8.7

Our Model Answers

1. Calculate the obtained scores for each student.

   To get obtained scores, we added the true score (X_t) to the corresponding error score (X_e). For example, for student 3, we added 24 to −6 and got 18.

2. Calculate the ΣX for each type of score.

   To get the sum of scores (ΣX) for each type of score, we added all the scores across the 10 students. For example, to arrive at the sum of the true scores, we added the scores for students 1 through 10 ($\Sigma X = 347$). Remember that when you sum error scores (X_e), the sum is always 0!

3. Calculate the M for each type of score.

   We calculated each of the three means (M) by dividing the each sum (ΣX) by 10 (the number of numbers we added up).

4. Calculate the σ^2 for each type of score.

   We calculated the standard deviation for each set of scores using our handy dandy computer program or calculator (aren't you glad we aren't making you calculate these by hand?). We squared the standard deviations to obtain the variances for each type of score. Review Chapter 3 if you have forgotten about standard deviations and variances.

5. Finally, check yourself to see whether the following equation is true for this set of data: $\sigma_o^2 = \sigma_t^2 + \sigma_e^2$

   You can check yourself by seeing if the variance of the true scores (64.21) plus the variance of the error scores (11.4) equals the variance of the obtained scores (75.61).

Student	True score X_t	Error Score X_e	Obtained Score X_o
1	46	−2	44
2	35	+4	39
3	24	−6	18
4	40	0	40
5	24	+6	30
6	35	−4	31
7	28	−1	27
8	28	+1	29
9	46	+2	48
10	41	0	41
$\Sigma X =$	347	0	347
$M =$	34.7	0.0	34.7
$\sigma^2 =$	64.21	11.4	75.61
$\sigma =$	8.01	3.38	8.7

Now It's Your Turn

Following is a set of data for you to play with.

Person	True score X_t	Error Score X_e	Obtained Score X_o
1	18	+2	
2	23	−5	
3	20	−1	
4	11	+3	
5	18	−2	
6	20	+1	
7	25	−4	
8	23	+5	
9	11	−3	
10	25	+4	
$\Sigma X =$			
$M =$			
$\sigma^2 =$			
$\sigma =$	4.8	3.3	5.9

1. Calculate the obtained scores for each person.

2. Calculate the ΣX for each type of score.

3. Calculate the M for each type of score.

4. Here is a gift: The standard deviation (σ) is given for each type of score. Now you calculate the σ^2 for each type of score.

5. Finally, check yourself to see whether the following equation is true for this set of data: $\sigma_o^2 = \sigma_t^2 + \sigma_e^2$

Our Model Answers

We have completed the table with the correct answers. How did you do?

Person	True score X_t	Error Score X_e	Obtained Score X_o
1	18	+2	**20**
2	23	−5	**18**
3	20	−1	**19**
4	11	+3	**14**
5	18	−2	**16**
6	20	+1	**21**
7	25	−4	**21**
8	23	+5	**28**
9	11	−3	**8**
10	25	+4	**29**
$\Sigma X =$	**194**	**0**	**194**
$M =$	**19.4**	**0.0**	**19.4**
$\sigma^2 =$	**23.44**	**11**	**34.44**
$\sigma =$	4.8	3.3	5.9

Words of Encouragement

Now that you understand basic test theory and can calculate some basic statistics related to test theory, you might be asking yourself, "So what?" This information is important because we want you to know that there is no such thing as absolute accuracy in measurement. If someone tells you they have an IQ of 146, you should be saying to yourself, "I wonder what their error score was!" In real life, we always want to consider that an obtained score is influenced by error. Therefore, when we use test scores to make decisions, we absolutely must be cautious.

Maybe the following example will demonstrate what we mean. Twin brothers took the same intelligence test to determine whether they would be placed in a gifted program. One brother scored two points higher than his twin. These two points placed him above the cutoff score and his parents were told he was accepted into the program for the gifted. His brother was not. The school personnel making this decision must have been ignorant (at least ignorant of test theory). Luckily for these boys, their parents refused to let the school discriminate between the twin brothers. The impact of not being placed in the gifted program for the one brother could have been devastating, could have pitted the brothers against each other, and could have had long-term psychological consequences for both brothers. This real life example drives home the point that when using obtained scores to make decisions about people's lives, we need to be cautious, fully informed, and humble.

What we have told you in this chapter is theoretical. You will never know someone's error score or true score. A major goal of testing is to minimize error so that obtained scores approach the true scores. You need to understand these concepts so that you do not treat obtained scores as if they were the truth. Measurement and testing are not infallible, so be cautious when drawing any conclusions about test scores or measurement data.

CHAPTER 8

Building a Strong Test—One the Big Bad Wolf Can't Blow Down

Building a test is like building a house—it is only as strong as the raw materials used to construct it. The "raw materials" used to build a test are the items. When constructing a test, your first job is to develop or write a pool of items. This is called *item generation*. To generate items, you have to be very familiar with the literature on the concept or focus of your test. If there is any theoretical foundation for the concept you're examining, you need to be familiar with this theory. Sometimes interviews with experts on the test topic or individuals experiencing the ramifications of the topic being examined will yield valuable information to help in item generation. When you generate items, you want a large pool of items so you can select the strongest items to build your test.

Here's an example of how one test was constructed. An issue important for retaining minority students on college campuses is their sense of fitting in culturally. However, no instrument or assessment device was found in 1995 that measured this concept. To build a strong instrument to measure "cultural congruity," the senior author of this text and another colleague thoroughly researched the literature, read extensively on theories related to college student retention, and interviewed racial or ethnic minority under-graduates. A pool of 20 items was generated and tested for their contribution to the Cultural Congruity Scale (CCS) (Gloria & Robinson Kurpius, 1996). The final scale consisted of only 13 items. Seven items from the original *item pool* were not good items and would have weakened the test. They were thrown out.

Whether standardized or "homemade," each test item has to make a significant contribution to the overall test. To determine whether an item is a "good" item and contributes to a strong test, each item is scrutinized. This scrutinization is like a building inspection that determines whether the building meets code. In measurement, this inspection is called *item analysis*. Item analysis is particularly essential for homemade tests such as those constructed for classroom use or for workplace use. Item analysis allows you to select or delete items in order to build a strong test—one that can't be blown apart or blown down.

Items can be analyzed qualitatively and quantitatively. Qualitative analysis looks at the content assessed by the item to ensure that the content matches the information, attitude, characteristic, or behavior being assessed. For example, if a social studies teacher, Ms. Government, had just taught a unit on the Constitution, her test should only ask questions about the material covered in this unit. If Ms. Government looks at each item on her test to check whether it reflects what she taught, she has done a qualitative item analysis. In contrast, a quantitative analysis looks at the statistical properties of each item. The two quantitative characteristics important for you to know are item difficulty and item discrimination.

Let's Check Your Understanding

1. Define item generation.

   _____

   _____

2. What is item analysis?

   _____

   _____

Our Model Answers

1. Define item generation.
   It is writing a large pool of items related to the concept being measured.

2. What is item analysis?
   It is a procedure to determine whether an item contributes to creating a strong test.

Item Difficulty

Typically, *item difficulty* for items with a dichotomous response format and scored right or wrong is defined as the percentage (or proportion p) of persons who get an item correct. The definition of item difficulty is more complex when there are multiple response options for an item, as in multiple-choice tests. It still refers to the number of people who got the item correct, but the actual formula (which we will not be teaching you) takes into consideration the number of response options.

The easier an item is, the larger the percentage of people who will get it correct. Like a percentage score, item difficulty (p) can range from 0 to 1.00. The larger the percentage of people who get the item correct, the larger the value of p.

To put this into context, let's look at Ms. Government's eighth-grade social studies class again. On her social studies quiz, 80% of her students got the item that asked about the three branches of government correct. The p for this item is 0.80. In contrast, only 15% ($p = 0.15$) correctly answered the item asking them about who signed the Constitution.

To determine whether an item's p value means that the item is a "strong" item or a "weak" one, we first need to think in terms of the purpose of the test. If Ms. Government wanted to test student mastery of information about the Constitution, she would love that 80% of her students knew that the government had three branches and would be very concerned that very few of her students knew who signed the Constitution. However, if her purpose was to select four students to compete in the state social studies competition, she would be most interested in the item that had an item difficulty of 0.15. She would want to identify those students who got this item correct as potential candidates for the competition. One item does not a building make, however. Ms. Government would want to look at all of the items that had a difficulty below $p = 0.50$ and pick the four students who most consistently got these items correct. The more difficult the item (the lower its p), the better this item discriminates between students who actually know the content being assessed and those who don't. Because we are interested in item difficulty, not item easiness, we need to think backward about values of p in order to discriminate between students who know the test content and those who don't.

Some Final Thoughts About Item Difficulty

Before we talk about item discrimination, however, a few more thoughts about item difficulty. **Thought One:** It would be nice if items on a test of knowledge were arranged from the easiest to the most difficult. We don't want people to be discouraged immediately; therefore, if most people get items at the beginning of the test correct, they might gain confidence. So, when you build a knowledge test, you may want to consider placing items with high *p* values first—that is, you use them for a foundation.

This brings us to **Thought Two**—Backward thinking: A low value for *p* reflects high item difficulty. A high value reflects low item difficulty.

Finally, **Thought Three** (we only had three thoughts, so we must not be very deep thinkers) has to do with item difficulty and the purpose of a test: If we want our test to discriminate among the people who take it, we don't want all items to have high *p* values. In contrast, if we're assessing content mastery, we don't want all items to have low *p* values. When the purpose of the test is to discriminate among those who take the test, the strongest tests have items with a spread of *p* values—some high, some low, and some in the middle. We want a test with an average item difficulty of approximately 0.50, because this maximizes the item true score variance (remember Chapter 7?). The closer the item difficulty is to 0 or 1.00, the lower the true score variance and the less accurate differential information it gives us about the people who took the test. Therefore, if our purpose is to discriminate, we include only a few items with extreme item difficulty values.

The closer the item difficulty is to 0.50, the more differentiations the item makes. An item difficulty of 0.50 indicates that half of the people being tested got it right and half got it wrong. Someone who truly knows the information will consistently get most items correct, regardless of item difficulty. In contrast, someone who doesn't know the information will consistently get most items wrong, except perhaps the items with high *p* values. This allows us to discriminate between those who have learned the information and those who haven't.

Now, if you do poorly on a test, you have to ask yourself: "Was this test too hard (all items had low *p* values), or did I really not understand all of the information being tested?" Your teacher is responsible for answering the first half of this question ("Was the test too hard?"). Remember what we said: A strong test has low, moderate, and high difficulty items. If the test is not strong (i.e., has weak items), the test should not have been used to assess your knowledge. You are responsible, however, for answering the second half of this question ("Did I really understand all of the information being tested?"). If the test is a strong test and you do poorly, don't blame the test.

 ## Let's Check Your Understanding

1. Define item difficulty.

   _____

   _____

2. Item difficulty scores can range from _____ to _____ .

Our Model Answers

1. Define item difficulty.
   Item difficulty is the percentage or portion of persons who get that item correct.

2. Item difficulty scores can range from **0** to **1.00.**

Item Discrimination

Throughout our discussion of item difficulty, we referred to the ability of a test to discriminate among people. A test cannot discriminate among people unless the items themselves differentiate between those who know the information being tested, have the attitude being assessed, or exhibit the behavior being measured and those who don't. Item discrimination is the "the degree to which an item differentiates correctly among test takers in the behavior that the test is designed to measure" (Anastasi & Urbina, 1997, p. 179).

What we want is for test items to discriminate between groups of people (often called *criterion groups*). Some potential criterion groups consist of those who succeed or fail in an academic course, in a training program, or in a job. As a budding measurement specialist, you need to be able to pick tests that have strong item discrimination (items that cannot be blown apart because they're not wishy-washy) or that help build a test with strong item discrimination ability. We want you to understand item discrimination conceptually, not necessarily calculate its statistical indices. Someday you might be asked to create a test, and we don't want you to forget the importance of item discrimination.

When creating or building your test, regardless of what you are trying to measure, you want each of your items to be able to discriminate between those who are high and low on whatever it is you are measuring. Even though an item has an acceptable item difficulty level, if it doesn't have the ability to discriminate, it is a weak item. It should not be included on the test. Lose it!!! Discard it!!! Get rid of it!!! Hide it in the refrigerator if you have to!!!

Just in case we're confusing you, maybe the following example will clear things up. You have a good job at a large utility company (lucky you) and one of your job responsibilities is recommending employees for promotion to middle-level managerial positions. In your company, a democratic leadership style is highly valued and has been found to be very effective with employees. Therefore, you always give those individuals being considered for promotion a leadership style instrument that assesses democratic and autocratic leadership styles. Every item on this instrument should be able to discriminate between those who would be democratic and those who would be autocratic managers.

When this leadership style instrument was originally validated (which we will explain in Chapter 10), it was administered to middle-level managers whose leadership style had been rated by their supervisors as democratic or autocratic. To determine whether an item had strong item discrimination, managers in the two leadership style groups needed to score differently on the item. For example, managers who had a democratic style would respond very positively to the item, "I involve employees in decision making." An autocratic leader would respond negatively to this item. Based on the different response patterns of democratic and autocratic managers, this item has strong item discrimination.

Ideally, the final version of the leadership style instrument does not include any items that do not discriminate between the two groups. Based on your validation study, you discarded those items earlier. If all items included on this test have good discriminating ability, you should be able to classify all your potential managers who respond consistently into two groups: democratic or autocratic.

We regret that we have to point out the vagaries of human nature. Some people will not respond consistently no matter how good the item discrimination is for every item on your test. Those people who answer inconsistently, sometimes agreeing with the democratic items and sometimes agreeing with the autocratic items, will have scores that reflect a mixed leadership style. The test items are not to blame for this confusion. Human inconsistency is to blame. We can't control everything. (Perhaps, a mixed leadership style is a good thing, too.)

Before we leave the topic of item discrimination, we feel compelled (as King Richard might say, "Nay, obligated!") to provide you with a wee bit of information about the *index of discrimination*. In our example of democratic and autocratic leadership styles, we used what is known as the *extreme groups* approach to item discrimination. To calculate the index of discrimination for each item for these two groups, you first calculate the percentage of managers who scored "democratic" on the item and the percentage of those who scored "autocratic" on the item. For this item, the difference (D) between these two percentages becomes its *index of discrimination*.

An index of discrimination can range from −1.00 to +1.00. The closer the D value comes to 0, the less discriminating ability the item has. In fact, $D = 0$ means no item discrimination. The closer the D value is to ±1.00, the stronger the item discrimination.

The exact formula for the index of discrimination is

$$D = U - L$$

The symbol U represents the percentage of people in one extreme group who endorsed the item. The symbol L represents the percentage of people in the other extreme group who also endorsed the item. Since we are interested in the democratic style, we are assigning U to the democratic leadership style group and L to the autocratic leadership style group. Table 8.1 presents data for these two groups on our eight-item Leadership Style Inventory.

Table 8.1   Computation of the Index of Discrimination

| | Percentage Passing | | |
Item	Democratic Style (U)	Autocratic Style (L)	Difference (Index of Discrimination)
1	80	25	55
2	55	50	5
3	75	20	55
4	30	70	−40
5	85	10	75
6	95	10	85
7	25	85	−60
8	15	70	−55

It would be nice if we could just interpret the D value in Table 8.1. However, D values are not independent of item difficulty and are biased in favor of moderately difficult items. What we can say from Table 8.1 is that item 2 has almost no item discrimination. Items 4, 7, and 8 were primarily endorsed by those with autocratic leadership styles, and items 1, 3, 5, and 6 were primarily endorsed by those with democratic leadership styles. These seven items have good discriminate ability. Item 2 is the "weakest link" and needs to be kicked out.

There are other indices of item discrimination that report the relationship between an item and some criterion that reflects what's being measured. These indices include the phi coefficient, the biserial correlation, and the point biserial correlation. If you are really interested in finding out more about these three, we suggest you take an advanced measurement course. An explanation of these three indices is beyond the scope of this "user friendly" text.

Let's Check Your Understanding

1. Define item discrimination.

_____

_____

2. Item discrimination scores can range from _____ to _____.

3. The index of discrimination is

_____

_____

 Our Model Answers

1. Define item discrimination.
   Item discrimination is the "the degree to which an item differentiates correctly among test takers in the behavior that the test is designed to measure" (Anastasi & Urbina, 1997, p. 179).

2. Item discrimination scores can range from **−1.00 to +1.00.**

3. The index of discrimination is **the difference (D) in the percentage of people in one extreme group minus the percentage of people in the other extreme group.**

Key Terms

- Item pool
- Item analysis
- Item difficulty
- Item discrimination
- Index of discrimination
- p value
- D value
- Extreme groups

Models and Self-instructional Exercises

Our Model

You have a 30-item test for which you have calculated item difficulty scores and an index of discrimination for each item.

1. One item has a difficulty level of $p = 0.35$. What does this mean conceptually?

_____

_____

2. Should this item be included on the test and why?

_____

_____.

3. If this is a strong test, the average item difficulty should be approximately _____.

4. An item with an index of discrimination of $D = 0.15$ indicates that

_____

_____.

5. Should this item be included on the test and why?

_____

_____

Our Model Answers

1. One item has a difficulty level of $p = 0.35$. What does this mean conceptually?

   An item with a difficulty level of $p = 0.35$ indicates that 35% of the people who took the test got this item correct.

2. Should this item be included on the test and why?

   It would be good to include this item on the test because it has moderate to high discriminating ability.

3. If this is a strong test, the average item difficulty should be approximately **0.50.**

4. An item with an index of discrimination of $D = 0.15$ indicates that **15% more people in the U group endorsed this item or got it correct than those in the L group.**

5. Should this item be included on the test and why?

   This item should not be included on the test, because its D value is relatively small and reflects little difference between the two groups. (Of course, we could make a better recommendation if we knew the item difficulty.)

 ## Now It's Your Turn

1. One item has a difficulty level of $p = 0.85$. What does this mean conceptually?

_____

_____

2. Should this item be included on the test and why?

_____

_____

3. An item with an index of discrimination of $D = -0.50$ indicates that

_____.

4. Should this item be included on the test and why?

_____

_____

 Our Model Answers

1. One item has a difficulty level of $p = 0.85$. What does this mean conceptually?

   An item with a difficulty level of $p = 0.85$ indicates that 85% of the people who took the test got this item correct.

2. Should this item be included on the test and why?

   This item may be too easy and not contribute to the item discrimination. We would only keep this item if there were also items with low p values to balance this item's high p value.

3. An item with an index of discrimination of $D = -0.50$ indicates that

   50% more people in the L group endorsed this item or got it correct than those in the U group.

4. Should this item be included on the test and why?

   This item should be included on the test, because its D value is relatively strong and reflects differences between the two groups. (Of course, we could make a more accurate recommendation if we knew the item difficulty.)

 Words of Encouragement

If you understand the material in this chapter and have grasped the material in the preceding seven chapters, we hope you are pleased with yourself. Even more, we hope that your exam grades reflect your understanding of this material.

CHAPTER 9

Reliability—The Same Yesterday, Today, and Tomorrow

When selecting tests for use either in research or in clinical decision making, you want to make sure that the tests you select are reliable. *Reliability* can be defined as the *trustworthiness* or the *accuracy* of a measurement. Those of us concerned with measurement issues also use the terms *consistency* and *stability* when discussing reliability. Consistency is the degree to which all parts of a test or different forms of a test measure the same thing. Stability is the degree to which a test measures the same thing at different times or in different situations. A reliability coefficient does not refer to the test as a whole, but it refers to scores obtained on a test. In measurement, we are interested in the consistency and stability of a person's scores.

As measurement specialists, we need to ask ourselves, "Is the score just obtained by Person X (Person X seems so impersonal; let's call her George) the same score she would get if she took the test tomorrow, or the next day, or the next week?" We want George's score to be a stable measure of her performance on any given test. The reliability coefficient is a measure of consistency. We also ask ourselves, "Is the score George received a true indication of her knowledge, ability, behavior, and so on?" Remember obtained scores, true scores, and error scores? The more reliable a test, the more George's obtained score is a reflection of her true score.

A reliability coefficient is a numerical value that can range from 0 to 1.00. A *reliability coefficient* of zero indicates the test scores are absolutely unreliable. In contrast, the higher the reliability coefficient, the more reliable or accurate the test scores. We want tests to have reliabilities above 0.70 for research purposes and in the 0.80s and 0.90s for clinical decision making. To compute a reliability coefficient, you must do one of three things:

1. Administer the test twice and keep track of the time interval between the two administrations.

2. Administer two different forms of the same test.

3. Administer the test one time.

More about this later.

Let's Check Your Understanding

1. The consistency or stability of test scores is called _____.

2. Does a reliability coefficient reflect
   a. Stability of a set of scores over time, or
   b. Stability of a set of scores across different tests?

3. When we say that reliability reflects accuracy of scores, do we mean
   a. How accurately the test measures a given concept, or
   b. How accurately the test measures the true score?

4. Reliability coefficients can range from _____ to _____.

5. When we are making clinical decisions (decisions about a person's life), we want the value of our reliability coefficients to be at least _____.

6. A test must always be administered twice in order for you to compute a reliability coefficient. True or false?

Our Model Answers

1. The consistency or stability of test scores is called **reliability.**

2. A reliability coefficient reflects the
   a. Stability of a set of scores over time

3. When we say that reliability reflects accuracy of scores, we mean
   b. How accurately the test measures the true score

4. Reliability coefficients can range from **0** to **+1.00.**

5. When we are making clinical decisions (decisions about a person's life), we want the value of our reliability coefficients to be at least **0.80.**

6. A test must always be administered twice in order for you to compute a reliability coefficient.
   This statement is false.

The Mathematical Foundation of Reliability

Now that you've mastered these basic concepts about reliability, we want to review quickly the concepts of obtained, true, and error score variance. Remember from classical test theory in Chapter 7 that it is assumed that the variance in obtained scores comprises true score variance and error score variance. One goal of measurement is to reduce as much error score variance as possible.

The equation $\sigma_o^2 = \sigma_t^2 + \sigma_e^2$ is key to understanding the concept of reliability. If we divide both sides of this equation by the obtained variance (σ_o^2), our equation is

$$1 = \frac{\sigma_t^2}{\sigma_o^2} + \frac{\sigma_e^2}{\sigma_o^2}$$

This equation shows us that the *ratio* of the true score variance to obtained score variance (σ_t^2/σ_o^2) plus the *ratio* of the error score variance to obtained score variance (σ_e^2/σ_o^2) sums to 1. The *ratio* of the true score variance to obtained score variance reflects the proportion of variance in obtained scores that are attributable to true scores. This concept is the basic definition of reliability. Therefore, we can substitute the symbol for reliability (r_{tt}) for (σ_t^2/σ_o^2) in the equation:

$$1 = r_{tt} + \frac{\sigma_e^2}{\sigma_o^2}$$

If we subtract the *ratio* of the error score variance to the obtained score variance (σ_e^2/σ_o^2), we have the basic formula for reliability:

$$r_{tt} = 1 - \frac{\sigma_e^2}{\sigma_o^2}$$

The closer the error variance comes to equaling 0, the closer the reliability coefficient comes to equaling 1.00. Error variance is never totally controlled, so it can never be equal to 0. This also means that the reliability will never be 1.00. At the risk of being redundant, in measurement we try to control as many sources of error variance as possible. To the extent that we can do this, the more accurately (reliably) we are measuring a person's true knowledge, behavior, personality, and so on.

Let's Check Your Understanding

Did you get all of that??? Check your understanding by answering the questions below.

1. Reliability is mathematically defined as the ratio of _____ variance in scores to the _____ variance.

2. The symbol we use for reliability is _____.

3. The lower the error variance, the _____ the reliability.

 ## Our Model Answers

1. Reliability is mathematically defined as the ratio of **true score** variance in scores to the **observed score** variance.

2. The symbol we use for reliability is r_{tt}.

3. The lower the error variance, the **higher** the reliability.

We are so proud of you! Thank you for hanging in with us.☺

Types of Reliability Estimates

Although there are a variety of types of reliability, we will only cover the four most important and most used. These four are *test–retest reliability, alternate forms reliability, internal consistency reliability,* and *interrater reliability.*

Test–Retest Reliability

This is the easiest to remember, because its name tells you exactly what you're doing. You're giving the test and then, after a designated time period, you're giving it again. The most common time periods are 1 week to 1 month. When test scores are reliable over time (i.e., good test–retest reliability), *error variance due to time* is controlled (as much as is possible). The statistical procedure used to examine test–retest reliability is correlation. A correlation coefficient tells us to what extent people obtain the same scores across the two testing times. The Pearson correlation coefficient is the statistic used to reflect test–retest reliability when total scores on a test are continuous.

Let's say that you are trying to create the *Flawless IQ Test.* Because you want it to compete with the Wechsler and Binet IQ tests, you create it with a mean of 100 and a *SD* of 15. You administer it to 100 sophomores (the human fruit flies) at the beginning of the semester. One month later you give it to them again. You correlate the students' scores on the first test with their scores when they took it the second time. In our example, the correlation coefficient you obtain is a measure of 1-month test–retest reliability for the Flawless IQ Test. To the extent that your students score the same on both tests, the higher the reliability coefficient. If your reliability coefficient is above 0.70, their scores are relatively stable over time (at least over 1 month). If your reliability coefficient is in the 0.80s or 0.90s, you have a better claim to stability because more error variance has been eliminated. Indeed, your reliability coefficient of 0.82 strongly suggests that this instrument reliably measures students' scores over a 1-month period.

Let's relook at the reliability of the Flawless IQ Test when we take race or ethnicity into consideration. You have 10 Latino students and 90 Euro-American students in your class. The scores for the 10 Latino students on each of the two test administrations are reported below.

Student	Score From Time 1	Score From Time 2
1	102	106
2	93	90
3	85	90
4	108	100
5	116	100
6	100	90
7	75	95
8	90	95
9	88	88
10	80	85

When the Pearson correlation coefficient is calculated for these 10 sets of scores, it is equal to 0.62. If we depicted this symbolically, it would look like this:

$$r_{\text{Time1*Time2}} = .62$$

This reliability coefficient indicates that your Flawless IQ Test is not so flawless. It may be stable across time for your Euro-American students, but it is not as stable for your Latino students. The poor reliability of scores for your Latino students may reflect cultural bias in your test. This reliability estimate of 0.62 suggests that you are not measuring IQ for these students very accurately. We'll discuss cultural bias in Chapter 11 on the ethics of testing.

Alternate Forms Reliability

This type of reliability is also known as *parallel forms reliability*. When you want to determine whether two equivalent forms of the same test are really equivalent, you calculate a correlation coefficient that is interpreted as alternate form reliability. In order for two forms to be parallel, they need to have the same number of items, test the same content, and have the same response format and options. Alternate forms of a test are usually given at two different times. The beauty of the alternate form procedure is that it helps to control for *sources of error due to both content variability and time.*

Maybe an example will help illustrate what we are talking about. For those of you who have taken aptitude tests such as the Millers Analogies Test (MAT), you may have discovered that there are multiple forms of the MAT (if you've taken it more than once to try to improve your score). The following 10 students took one form of the MAT in January and a different form of the MAT in May. Here are their scores:

Student	MAT Score From January	MAT Score From May
1	50	52
2	35	45
3	42	40
4	68	74
5	73	80
6	52	50
7	79	80
8	60	61
9	59	67
10	48	55

The alternate forms reliability coefficient for these scores across this 4-month period is 0.95. If we depicted this symbolically, it would look like this:

$$r_{Form1 \cdot Form2} = .95$$

The measurement specialists who designed these alternate forms of the MAT did a great job. (Let's hope they were given a bonus for a job well done!) This 0.95 is a very strong reliability coefficient and indicates that sources of error due to both content variability and time were controlled to a very great extent.

Internal Consistency Reliability

This type of reliability is a bird of a different color. It does not require two testing times or two forms of a test. You administer the test one time, and you let the computer find the mean of the correlations among all possible halves of the test. This procedure is also called a *split-half procedure*. What you are trying to find out is whether every item on the test correlates with every other item. You are assessing *content stability.*

Let's look at an example of a five-item test designed to measure *Personal Valuing of Education.* The five items are

1. How strong is your commitment to earning a bachelor's degree?

2. Getting a college degree will be worth the time required to obtain it.

3. Getting a college degree will be worth the money spent to obtain it.

4. Getting a college degree will be worth the work/effort required to get it.

5. How much do you value a college education?

The continuous response format ranges from 1 (not at all/strongly disagree) to 5 (very much/strongly agree). Did you remember that this is called a continuous response format because there are more than two response options for each item? The responses for 10 students to each of these items are presented in Table 9.1.

Table 9.1 Continuous Responses to the Personal Valuing of Education Scale

Student	Item 1	Item 2	Item 3	Item 4	Item 5
1	4	3	4	4	5
2	3	3	3	3	3
3	2	4	4	4	3
4	1	2	1	2	2
5	3	4	4	4	5
6	2	3	2	4	2
7	3	3	4	4	4
8	4	4	3	3	4
9	3	3	2	2	3
10	4	4	4	3	4

Because this test used a continuous response format, the type of internal consistency reliability coefficient we calculated was a Cronbach's alpha. With the assistance of the Scale option in SPSS, we found that the Cronbach's alpha for responses to these five items was 0.87. This suggests that for each student, their responses to each of the items were very similar. An internal consistency reliability coefficient of 0.87 is considered relatively strong and suggests that these five items are measuring the same content.

If you want to check our accuracy, open the Personal Valuing of Education data set on the Sage Web site at www.sagepub.com/kurpius. Under Analyze, choose Scale, then choose Reliability Analysis. From the window that opens, select and move the five test items from the left to the right using the arrow. Then click Statistics and check all of the Descriptives in the next window. Click Continue and then OK. You will get results that look like ours in Figure 9.1.

Reliability Statistics

Cronbach's Alpha	N of Items
.869	5

Figure 9.1   Cronbach's Alpha Reliability Output

What should we have done if the response options had been dichotomous? Instead of being able to rate the items on a scale from 1 to 5, the students had only two choices, such as yes/no or none/a lot. Table 9.2 presents these same students but the response option was dichotomous. Scores of 1 reflect responses of "no" or "none" and scores of 2 reflect "yes" or "a lot."

Table 9.2   Dichotomous Responses to the Personal Valuing of Education Scale

Student	Item 1	Item 2	Item 3	Item 4	Item 5
1	2	2	2	2	2
2	1	2	1	2	1
3	1	2	1	2	2
4	1	1	1	1	1
5	2	2	2	2	2
6	1	2	1	2	1
7	2	2	1	2	2
8	2	2	1	2	2
9	2	2	1	1	2
10	2	2	2	2	2

When students were forced to use a dichotomous response format, the internal consistency reliability coefficient was 0.78. This is a moderately acceptable reliability coefficient. Based on this internal consistency reliability of 0.78, you can conclude that the students tended to respond consistently to the five items on the *Personal Valuing of Education* scale.

The statistical procedure that was used to arrive at this coefficient is called the *Kuder-Richardson 20* (K-R 20). The K-R 20 should only be used with dichotomous data. When using SPSS to calculate a K-R 20, you should click Analyze, then select Scales, then choose Reliability Analysis, and then choose the Alpha option for this analysis. (Kuder and Richardson also developed the K-R 21, but it is not generally as acceptable as the K-R 20.)

Because an internal consistency reliability coefficient is based on dividing the test in half in order to correlate it with the other half, we have artificially shortened the test. A 20-item test became two 10-item tests. When a test is too short, the reliability coefficient is suppressed due to the statistics that are employed. A *Spearman-Brown correction* procedure can be used to compensate for this artificial shortening. The Spearman-Brown should only be used with internal consistency reliability. If you see it reported for either test–retest or alternate forms reliability, the writer didn't know what he or she was talking about.

A final note about internal consistency reliability—never use it with a speeded test. Speeded tests are designed so that they cannot be finished. Therefore, calculating reliability based on halves produces a worthless reliability coefficient.

Interrater Reliability

This fourth type of reliability is used when two or more raters are making judgments about something. For example, let's say you are interested in whether a teacher consistently reinforces students' answers in the classroom. You train two raters to judge a teacher's response to students as reinforcing or not reinforcing. They each observe the same teacher at the same time and code the teacher's response to a student as reinforcing (designated by an X) or not reinforcing (designated by an O). The two raters' judgments might look like the following:

Teacher Responses	Rater 1	Rater 2
1	X	X
2	X	0
3	0	0

(Continued)

Teacher Responses	Rater 1	Rater 2
4	X	X
5	0	0
6	X	X
7	X	X
8	X	X
9	0	X
10	0	0

To calculate interrater reliability, you count the number of times the raters agreed and divide by the number of possible times they could have agreed. The formula for this is:

$$\text{Interrater reliability} = \frac{\text{Number of agreements}}{\text{Number of possible agreements}}$$

$$\text{Interrater reliability} = \frac{8}{10} = 0.80$$

The interrater reliability coefficient for these two raters is 0.80. They tended to view the teacher's behavior in a similar fashion. If you want your reliability coefficient to be stronger, have them discuss the two responses that they viewed differently and come to some consensus about what they are observing. Another commonly used statistic for interrater reliability is the Cohen's Kappa.

 ## Let's Check Your Understanding

OK, friends, have you digested this yet or has it left a bad taste in your mouth? It's time to check your understanding of types of reliability by answering the questions below.

1. What are the four major types of reliability?

_____

_____

2. Which type is designed to control for error due to time?

_____

_____

3. Which type is designed to control for error due to time and content?

_____

_____

4. For which type do you need to administer the test only one time?

_____

_____

5. What happens to the reliability coefficient when it is based on halves of a test?

_____

_____

6. How do you calculate interrater reliability?

_____

_____

Our Model Answers

We suggest that you pay close attention. In our answers, we're throwing in bits of new information that your instructor may well hold you accountable for on your exam.

1. What are the four major types of reliability?
   Test-retest, alternate forms, internal consistency, and interrater reliabilities.

2. Which type is designed to control for error due to time?
   Test-retest reliability controls for error due to time, because the test is administered at two different time periods. The time period between the two testings indicates the length of time that the test scores have been found to be stable.

3. Which type is designed to control for error due to time and content?
   Alternate forms reliability controls for error due to time and content. It controls for the exact time period between the two testings as well as the equivalency of item content across the two forms of the test.

4. For which type do you need to administer the test only one time?

   You only need to administer a test once if you are calculating internal consistency reliability. This type of reliability only controls for sources of error due to content since no time interval is involved.

5. What happens to the reliability coefficient when it is based on halves of a test?

   If the length of the possible halves of a test contains too few items, the reliability coefficient may be distorted and typically is too small. The Spearman-Brown correction somewhat compensates for this statistical artifact.

6. How do you calculate interrater reliability?

   You divide the number of agreements for the two raters by the number of possible agreements to get interrater reliability.

Standard Error of Measurement

Any discussion of reliability would be incomplete if *standard error of measurement* (SE_m) was not discussed. Standard error of measurement is directly related to reliability. The formula for standard error of measurement is

$$SE_m = SD_o \sqrt{1 - r_{tt}}$$

The more reliable your test scores, the smaller your SE_m. For example, let's say your reliability is 0.90 and the SD_o is 3 (SD_o is the standard deviation for the test). If these values are inserted in the formula, your SE_m is 0.95. If your reliability is 0.70, your SE_m is 1.64. The higher the reliability, the less error in your measurement. Here's how we arrived at our two answers.

$$SE_m = SD_o \sqrt{1 - r_{tt}} \qquad SE_m = SD_o \sqrt{1 - r_{tt}}$$
$$SE_m = 3 \sqrt{1 - .90} \qquad SE_m = 3 \sqrt{1 - .70}$$
$$SE_m = 3 \sqrt{.1} \qquad SE_m = 3 \sqrt{.3}$$
$$SE_m = .95 \qquad SE_m = 1.64$$

A standard error of measurement is a deviation score and reflects the area around an obtained score where you would expect to find the true score. This area is called a *confidence interval.* Yeah, that sounds like gobbledygook to us too. Perhaps an example might clarify what we are trying to say.

Mary, one of our star pupils, obtained a score of 15 on our first measurement quiz. If the reliability coefficient for this quiz was 0.90, the SE_m is 0.95. Mary's obtained score of 15 could be viewed as symbolizing the mean of all possible scores Mary could receive on this test if she took it over and over and over. An obtained score is analogous to a mean on the normal, bell-shaped curve, and the SE_m is equivalent to a SD. Mary's true score would be within $\pm 1 SE_m$ of her obtained score 68.26% of the time ($X_o \pm 1 SE_m$). That is, we are 68.26% confident that Mary's true score would fall between the scores 14.05 and 15.95. We got these numbers by subtracting 0.95 from Mary's score of 15 and by adding 0.95 to Mary's score of 15. Remember, it helps to think of Mary's obtained score as representing the mean and the SE_m as representing a SD on a normal curve.

Surprise, surprise: Mary's true score would be within $\pm 2 SE_m$ of her obtained score 95.44% of the time—between the scores of 13.10 and 16.90. If you guessed that Mary's true score would be within $\pm 3 SE_m$ of her obtained score 99.74% of the time (between 12.15 and 17.85), you are so smart. If you remembered standard deviation from Chapter 4, this was a piece of cake for you.

Let's see what happens when the reliability is only 0.70. As we calculated above, the SE_m is 1.64. Mary still received an obtained score of 15. We can be confident 68.26% of the time that Mary's true score is within $\pm 1 SE_m$ of this obtained score (between scores of 13.36 and 16.64). Mary's true score would be within $\pm 2 SE_m$ of her obtained score 95.44% of the time—between a score of 11.72 and a score of 18.28. By now you know that Mary's true score would be within $\pm 3 SE_m$ of this obtained score 99.74% of the time (between 10.08 and 19.72).

Notice that when the test has a high reliability as in the first case, we are more confident that the value of Mary's true score is closer to her obtained score. The SE_m is smaller, which reflects a smaller error score. Remember that a goal in reliability is to control error.

Let's Check Your Understanding

1. What is the mathematical symbol for standard error of measurement?

   _____

2. What is the relationship between standard error of measurement and a reliability coefficient?

   _____

   _____

3. What does a 68.26% confidence interval mean?

   _____

   _____

4. If Mary in our example above had obtained a score of 18, and the SE_m was 4, her true score would be between what two scores at the 95.44% confidence interval?

_____

_____

 Our Model Answers

1. What is the mathematical symbol for standard error of measurement?
   SE_m

2. What is the relationship between standard error of measurement and a reliability coefficient?
   They have a negative relationship. The greater the reliability coefficient, the smaller the standard error of measurement.

3. What does a 68.26% confidence interval mean?
   A 68.26% confidence interval indicates that you can expect to find the true score within $\pm 1 SE_m$ from the obtained score.

4. If Mary in our example above had obtained a score of 18, and the SE_m was 4, her true score would be between what two scores at the 95.44% confidence interval?
   The two scores are 10 and 26. We arrived at these scores by adding and subtracting $2 SE_m$ to the obtained score of 18. The mathematical value of $2 SE_m$ was $2(4) = 8$.

Correlation Coefficients as Measures of Reliability

We've already told you that the Pearson product-moment correlation is used to assess test–retest and alternate forms reliability because total test scores are continuous data and reflect interval-level data. When we look at individual items to assess internal consistency reliability, we use either the Cronbach's alpha for continuous response formats or the K-R 20 for dichotomous response formats. Before we end this chapter, we need to comment on what type of reliability you would use for ordinal or rank-ordered data. Ranked data might include placement in class or teacher's ratings of students (first, second, third, etc.). The correct procedure for rank-ordered data is the *Spearman rho*.

Some Final Thoughts About Reliability

There are several principles that we need to keep in mind about reliability:

1. When administering a test, follow the instructions carefully so that your administration matches that of anyone else who would be administering this same test. This controls for one source of error.

2. Try to establish standardized testing conditions such as good lighting in the room, freedom from noise, and other environmental conditions. These can all be sources of error.

3. Reliability is affected by the length of a test, so make sure you have a sufficient number of items to reflect the true reliability.

Key Terms

- Reliability
  - Test–retest
  - Alternate forms
  - Internal consistency
  - Interrater
- Standard error of measurement
- Pearson product-moment correlations
- K-R 20
- Cronbach's alpha
- Spearman-Brown correction

Models and Self-instructional Exercises

Our Model

Business and industry are increasingly concerned about employee theft. To help identify potential employees who may have a problem with honesty, you have created the Honesty Inventory (HI). You have normed it on employees representative of different groups of workers, such as used car salesmen, construction workers, lawyers, and land developers. You have been asked to assess applicants for bank teller positions. You know that the 2-week test–retest reliability of the HI scores for bank tellers is 0.76. You administer the HI to the applicants. The applicants' scores range from 20 to 55 out of a possible 60 points. Their mean score is 45 with a standard deviation of 2.

1. What is the SE_m for this group of applicants?

$$SE_m = SD_o \sqrt{1 - r_{tt}}$$

2. One applicant, Tom, scored 43. At a 95% confidence level, between what two scores does his true score lie?

   Between _____ and _____.

3. Based on what you know so far about Tom and the other applicants, would you recommend him as an employee? Yes or no?

4. Why did you make this recommendation?

   _____

   _____

   _____

5. When you calculated the internal consistency for this group of applicants, the Cronbach's alpha reliability coefficient was 0.65. What does this tell you about the content of the HI for these applicants?

   _____

   _____

   _____

 Our Model Answers

Being conscientious measurement consultants, we want to be conservative in our opinions. Therefore, we pay close attention to our data when making recommendations. To err is human, but in business they don't forgive.

1. What is the SE_m for this group of applicants?

$$SE_m = SD_o \sqrt{1 - r_{tt}}$$
$$SE_m = 2 \sqrt{1 - .76}$$
$$SE_m = 2 \sqrt{.24}$$
$$SE_m = .98$$

2. One applicant, Tom, scored 43. At a 95% confidence level, between what two scores does his true score lie?

   We are confident 95% of the time that Tom's true score is between 41.04 and 44.96.

3. Based on what you know so far about Tom and the other applicants, would you recommend him as an employee?

   We would not recommend Tom for employment.

4. Why did you make this recommendation?

   At the 95th confidence level, Tom's highest potential true score is still barely equal to the mean score of 45 for this applicant pool. More than likely, his true score is significantly below the group mean. We would look for applicants whose true score would at a minimum include the mean and scores above it at the 95% confidence interval.

5. When you calculated the internal consistency reliability for this group of applicants, the Cronbach's alpha reliability coefficient was 0.65. What does this tell you about the content of the HI for these applicants?

   A 0.65 internal consistency reliability coefficient indicates that the applicants did not respond consistently to all the items on the HI. This suggests significant content error. We need to tread very lightly in making any recommendations about this group of applicants based on the internal consistency reliability for the HI for their scores. Remember that the reliability coefficient is suppressed when a test is shortened, as happens when internal consistency reliability is calculated.

Now It's Your Turn

The same applicants are also given a multidimensional test that assesses both interpersonal relationships (IP) and fear of math (FOM). For a norm group of 500 business majors, the reported Cronbach's alpha across their 30-item IP scores was 0.84. Their K-R 20 was 0.75 across their 30-item FOM scores. For the bank teller applicants, their mean score on the IP subscale is 50 ($SD = 4$, possible score range 0 to 60, with higher scores reflecting stronger interpersonal skills). Their mean score on the FOM subscale is 20 ($SD = 2.2$, possible score range 0 to 30, with higher scores reflecting greater fear of math).

1. What is the SE_m for each subscale for this group of applicants?

$$SE_m = SD_o \sqrt{1 - r_{tt}}$$

Interpersonal Relationships Subscale	Fear of Math Subscale

2. One applicant, Harold, scored 50 on the IP subscale. At a 68.26% confidence level, between what two scores does his true score lie?

   Between _____ and _____.

3. Harold scored 10 on the FOM subscale. At a 68.26% confidence level, between what two scores does his true score lie?

   Between _____ and _____.

4. Based on what you know so far about Harold on these two subscales, would you recommend him as an employee? Yes or no?

5. Why did you make this recommendation?

   _____

   _____

   _____

   _____

6. Six months later you retested the candidates you hired. The test–retest reliability coefficient was 0.88 for the IP scores and was 0.72 for FOM scores. What does this tell you about the stability of the two subscales?

   _____

   _____

   _____

   _____

Our Model Answers

1. What is the SE_m for each subscale for this group of applicants?

Interpersonal Relationships Subscale	Fear of Math Subscale
$SE_m = SD_o \sqrt{1 - r_{tt}}$ $SE_m = 4\sqrt{1 - .84}$ $SE_m = 1.6$	$SE_m = SD_o \sqrt{1 - r_{tt}}$ $SE_m = 2.2\sqrt{1 - .75}$ $SE_m = 1.1$

2. One applicant, Harold, scored 50 on the IP subscale. At a 68.26% confidence level, between what two scores does his true score lie?

    Between 48.4 and 51.6. To get these two values, we added and subtracted 1.6 (the SE_m) from Harold's score of 50.

3. Harold scored 10 on the FOM subscale. At a 68.26% confidence level, between what two scores does his true score lie?

    Between 8.9 and 11.1. To get these two values, we added and subtracted 1.1 (the SE_m) from Harold's score of 10.

4. Based on what you know so far about Harold on these two subscales, would you recommend him as an employee?

    Yes, we should hire him.

5. Why did you make this recommendation?

    Based only on these two tests, we chose to hire Harold because he has average interpersonal skills and low fear of math. His scores on these two measures suggest that he will interact satisfactorily with others (with customers as well as coworkers) and he will be comfortable dealing with the mathematics related to being a bank teller (we don't know his actual math ability, however).

6. Six months later you retested the candidates you hired. The test–retest reliability coefficient was 0.88 for the IP scores and was 0.68 for FOM scores. What does this tell you about the stability of the two subscales?

    The interpersonal relationships subscale scores were quite stable over a 6-month time period for the pool of bank teller applicants who were actually hired. The scores on the fear of math subscale for those who were hired were not as stable across time. This might be due to the restricted range that resulted if only those with lower fear of math scores on the initial testing were actually hired. The test-retest reliability coefficient of 0.68 might also be related to the fact that the K-R 20 was also relatively low (0.75).

Words of Encouragement

Do you realize that you have successfully completed almost all of this book? Mastering the content in this chapter is a major accomplishment. We hope you are starting to see how the measurement issues in the earlier chapters have applicability for this more advanced topic—reliability.

If you want to practice using SPSS to calculate reliability coefficients, we suggest you visit www.sagepub.com/kurpius. Individual test item responses for six different tests for 270 undergraduates can be found in the *Measurement Data Set*.

CHAPTER 10

Validity—What You See Is Not Always What You Get

Suppose you've created a test that has perfect reliability ($r = +1.00$). Anyone who takes this test gets the same score time after time after time. The obtained score is their true score. There is no error. Well, doesn't this sound wonderful!? Don't be gullible. If you believe there is such a thing as a perfectly reliable test, could we interest you in some ocean-front property in the desert? Remember that "what you see is not always what you get."

We're sorry to tell you, but having a perfectly reliable test is not enough. Indeed, a perfectly reliable test (or even a nonreliable test) may not have any value at all. We offer the case of Professor Notsobright to prove our point. Professor Notsobright wants to know how smart or intelligent everyone in his class is. He knows that intelligence is related to the brain and decides, therefore, that brain size must surely reflect intelligence. Since he can't actually measure brain size, he measures the circumference of each student's head. Sure enough, he gets the same values each time he takes out his handy-dandy tape measure and encircles each student's head. He has found a reliable measurement. What he has NOT found is a *valid measure* of the construct *intelligence*.

In measurement, our objective is to use tests that are valid as well as reliable. This chapter introduces you to the most fundamental concept in measurement—*validity*. Validity is defined as how well a test measures what it is designed to measure. In addition, validity tells us what can be inferred from test scores. According to the *Standards for Educational and Psychological Testing* (1999), "the process of validation involves accumulating evidence to provide a sound scientific basis for the proposed score interpretations" (p. 9). Evidence of validity is related to the accuracy of the proposed interpretation of test scores, not to the test itself.

Good ol' Professor Notsobright wanted to measure the construct of intelligence. The approach he mistakenly chose (measuring the circumference of his students' heads) does not yield valid evidence of intelligence. He would be totally wrong to interpret any scores he obtained as an indicator of his students' intelligence. (We think Professor Notsobright got his degree through a mail-order catalog. Furthermore, we suggest that someone who knows about validity assess Dr. Notsobright's intelligence and suggest he seek different employment.)

Scores on a test need to be valid and reliable. Evidence of validity is typically reported as a *validity coefficient,* which can range from 0 to +1.00. Like the reliability coefficient discussed in Chapter 9, a validity coefficient is often a correlation coefficient. A validity coefficient of 0 indicates the test scores absolutely do not measure the construct under investigation. A validity coefficient approaching +1.00 (which you probably will never see in your lifetime) provides strong evidence that the test scores are measuring the construct under investigation.

Ideally, test developers should report a validity coefficient for each of the groups for which the test could be used. That is, if you're going to give an achievement test to middle school students, a validity coefficient for each middle school grade level should be reported. In addition, validity coefficients for boys and for girls within each grade level should be reported. Remember when we talked about norm groups in Chapter 6? Well, in a perfect measurement world, validity coefficients would be reported for all the potential groupings discussed in that chapter.

The test user also has responsibility for test validation. If the test is going to be used in a setting different from that reported by the test developers, the user is responsible for evaluating the validity evidence in the new setting. For example, if a test was originally validated with public school students, but you want to use it with students in a private parochial school, you have a responsibility for providing evidence of validity in this new school setting.

Regardless of how evidence of validity is established, we want to stress that validity is a theoretical concept. It can never actually be measured. A validity coefficient only suggests that test scores are valid for certain groups in certain circumstances under certain conditions. We *never ever* "prove" validity, no matter how hard we try. In spite of this, validity is an absolutely essential characteristic of a strong test. Only when a test is valid (and of course, reliable) will you "get what you see."

 ## Let's Check Your Understanding

It's time to check your understanding of what we've told you so far.

1. *Validity* is defined as _____.

2. When interpreting a test score, what is the role of validity?

   _____

   _____

3. Validity coefficients can range in value from _____ to _____.

4. When we talk about validity, are we referring to a test's scores or the test itself?

   _____

5. Test scores need to be both _____ and _____.

6. If we try hard enough, we can prove that the test scores are valid. True or false?

 Our Model Answers

1. *Validity* is defined as **how well a test measures what it is designed to measure.**

2. When interpreting a test score, what is the role of validity?
   Validity tells us what can be inferred from test scores.

3. Validity coefficients can range in value from **0 to +1.00.**

4. When we talk about validity, are we referring to a test's scores or the test itself?
   When we talk about validity, we are referring to a test's scores. Evidence of validity allows us to make accurate interpretation of someone's test score. We do not interpret a test.

5. Test scores need to be both **valid** and **reliable.**

6. If we try hard enough, we can prove that the test scores are valid.
   This statement is false. Since validity is a theoretical concept, you can never prove its existence.

Helping You Get What You See

Like the Phantom of the Opera whose presence hovers over and shapes the meaning of Andrew Lloyd Webber's musical, validity hovers over and shapes the meaning of a test. As the musical evolves, the phantom becomes more visible; as more evidence of validity evolves, the meaning of test scores becomes clearer. To develop evidence of validity, attention needs to be given to validation groups, criteria, construct underrepresentation, and construct-irrelevant variance.

Validation Groups

The groups on which a test is validated are called *validation groups.* For our achievement test example, the validation groups were middle school students. The achievement test is valid for students who have the same characteristics as those in the validation sample of middle school students. Anyone who will potentially use this achievement test needs to determine how closely his or her students match the characteristics of the students in the validation group. The more dissimilar the students are from the validation group, the less valid the achievement test may be for the new group of students. Characteristics of the validation group should be presented in a test's manual.

Criteria

Validity is always a reflection of some *criterion* against which it is being measured. A criterion is some knowledge, behavior, skill, process, or characteristic that is not a component of the test being examined. It is external to the test itself. For example, scores on the Scholastic Aptitude Test (SAT) or the Graduate Record Examination (GRE) have typically been validated against the criterion of undergraduate grade point averages (GPA) or grades in graduate school, respectively. A fairly strong positive relationship has been found between scores on these tests and later GPAs (the criteria).

Scores on a test may also be validated against multiple criteria, depending on the inferences to be made from the test scores. For example, scores on the Goody-Two-Shoes (G2S) personality test, which measures a complex construct, probably need to be validated against several criteria. Appropriate criteria might include teachers' perceptions of students, interpersonal relationships, potential for career success, and so forth. Each of these criteria helps to define the goody-two-shoes construct. There would be a separate validity coefficient for the relationship between the scores of the G2S test and each of these criteria. Collectively, these validity coefficients provide evidence for the validity of the G2S scores measuring the construct *"goody-two-shoes."*

In addition, based on which criterion was used to gather validity evidence, the interpretation of the G2S test scores would vary. One would suspect, at least we do, that there may be a strong correlation between students being "goody-two-shoes" and teachers' very favorable perceptions of these students. Therefore, the criterion of teachers' perceptions of students provides strong evidence for the validity of scores on the G2S test as a measure of teachers' perceptions of students. The same type of evidence needs to be gathered on the other criteria in order to interpret scores on the G2S test as reflecting these criteria.

Construct Underrepresentation

When a test fails to capture or assess all important aspects of a construct adequately, this is called *construct underrepresentation*. Let's go back to our example of aptitude tests to illustrate construct underrepresentation. Most of you have probably taken the SAT or GRE. Furthermore, a few of you have probably argued that your SAT or GRE test scores did not accurately reflect your academic ability. You may not know this, but it really is possible that some tests don't comprehensively measure the constructs they are designed to measure. When this happens, these tests are suffering from a serious illness that could even be fatal—construct underrepresentation.

Let's pretend that the GRE suffers from construct underrepresentation. It doesn't really, but our example will make more sense if we pretend that it does. Traditionally, the GRE measured quantitative and verbal aptitude. More recently, reasoning ability was added to the GRE to complement its assessment of quantitative and verbal abilities. Perhaps the test developers realized that the original GRE measured aptitude too narrowly, so they added items to broaden the measure to include reasoning ability. Doing this broadened the domain of behaviors that reflect aptitude. Perhaps, this more comprehensive assessment allows the GRE items to better represent the construct *aptitude*.

Construct-Irrelevant Variance

It is also possible that when you took the SAT or GRE some process extraneous to the test's intended construct affected the test scores. These extraneous variables might include things such as your reading ability, speed of reading, emotional reactions to test items, familiarity with test content, test anxiety, or items not related to the construct(s) being measured. Each of these can contribute to *construct-irrelevant variance*. This is a source of error in the validity coefficient.

Before we introduce you to the most common sources of validity evidence, it's time to check your understanding of the concepts just introduced.

Let's Check Your Understanding

1. The individuals to be tested need to have characteristics similar to those of the _____.

2. A criterion is _____.

3. A test should be validated against one and only one criterion. True or false?

4. The criteria used as a source of validity evidence are external to the test itself. True or false?

5. Construct underrepresentation occurs when _____ _____.

6. A source of error in a validity coefficient that is not related to the test's intended construct is called _____.

7. Examples of this source of error include _____ and _____.

Our Model Answers

1. The individuals to be tested need to have characteristics similar to those of the **validation group.**

2. A criterion is **some knowledge, behavior, skill, process, or characteristic that is used to establish the validity of test scores.**

3. A test should be validated against one and only one criterion.
   This statement is false. Test scores should be validated on as many criteria as are relevant to the construct being measured. Multiple sources of validity evidence are particularly needed when the test measures a complex construct.

4. The criteria used as a source of validity evidence are external to the test itself.
   True. Criteria are not components of the test itself.

5. Construct underrepresentation occurs when **the test does not adequately assess all aspects of the construct being measured.**

6. A source of error in a validity coefficient that is not related to the test's intended construct is called **construct-irrelevant variance.**

7. Examples of this source of error include **reading ability, speed of reading, emotional reactions to test items, familiarity with test content, test anxiety, or items not related to the construct(s) being measured.**

Sources of Validity Evidence

If you read the measurement literature (don't laugh, we find some of this literature very interesting), you might have noticed that multiple "types" of validity are presented. Most likely, you'll find the terms *content, construct, concurrent,* and *predictive validity*. Based on the *Standards for Educational and Psychological Testing* (1999), validity is viewed as a unitary concept. It is the extent to which all sources of evidence for validity support the intended interpretation of test scores. Even though validity is indeed a unitary concept, you still need to know about the traditional types or sources of evidence for validity.

Evidence Based on Test Content

Examination of the content covered by test items and the construct the test is intended to measure can yield important evidence for *content validity*. Test developers typically write their items to reflect a specific content domain. Examples of test content domains might include the Revolutionary War, measures of central tendency, eating disorders, leadership style, or star constellations. The more clearly every item on a test taps information from one specific content domain, the greater the evidence for content validity.

Evidence for content validity typically comes from two approaches: (1) an empirical analysis of how well the test items reflect the content domain and (2) expert ratings of the relationship between the test items and the content domain. Empirical evidence can be derived from a statistical procedure such as factor analysis to determine whether all of the test items measure one content domain or construct. The second approach, expert ratings, requires identification of people who are experts on a content area. These experts then jointly agree on the parameters of the content domain or construct they will be evaluating. Finally, based on these parameters, they judge each item as to how well it assesses the desired content.

Content validity is most easily illustrated with an example from education. Every test you have taken, whether in your math classes, your English classes, or this measurement class, should only include items that assess the content or information covered in that class. This information may have been given through lectures, readings, discussions, or demonstrations. The professor, who is the content expert, develops the class tests by creating items that reflect the specific information covered in the course. To the extent that the content of all of the items reflect the course content, evidence of content validity is established. Items that do not reflect the course content contribute to *construct-irrelevant variance*. These items cause variation in test scores that is not related to knowledge of the course content. Not all professors know about construct-irrelevant variance—they may or may not appreciate your educating them. So, use your knowledge wisely. (Believe it or not, even professors can become defensive.)☺

In the world of work, evidence of content validity is provided by a strong correspondence between specific job tasks and the content of test items. Experts identify the dimensions of a job or the tasks that the job comprises. One process of deriving job tasks is to observe job behaviors systematically. Test items are then evaluated against the specific job tasks. The correspondence between the test items and the job tasks is referred to as the *job relatedness* of the test. Indeed, the U.S. Supreme Court has mandated that tests used for job selection or placement have job relatedness.

The appropriateness of a specific content domain is directly related to any interpretation or inferences to be made from test scores. In our education example, we may want to draw conclusions about individual student mastery of a content area such as knowledge of star constellations. Based on their level of mastery, we may want to make decisions about students passing or not passing the class.

We may also want to interpret test scores to find areas of a curriculum being adequately or inadequately taught. If the majority of students systematically miss items related to class content, then perhaps this content was not adequately taught. If we had given the students a comprehensive achievement test that was designed and validated to measure multiple dimensions of achievement, we could draw conclusions about content neglected or content taught based on student responses to test items. Information about content neglected and about content taught both provide evidence of content validity.

Evidence of Criterion-Related Validity

A second "type" or source of validity evidence is *criterion-related validity*. If the purpose of a test is to predict some future behavior or to estimate current behavior, you want evidence that the test items will do this accurately. The relationship between test scores and the variable(s) external to the test (criterion) will provide this source of evidence for criterion-related validity, as discussed next.

Predictive and Concurrent Validity

If the goal is for test scores to *predict future behavior*, we are concerned with *predictive validity*. This source of evidence indicates that the test scores are strongly related to (predict) some behavior (criterion) that is measured at a later time. Remember our example of the SAT and GRE aptitude tests? The ability of scores on these two tests to predict future GPAs accurately provides evidence for their predictive validity.

In contrast, evidence for *concurrent validity* indicates a strong relationship between test scores and some criterion measured *at the same time*. Both assessments are administered concurrently (or in approximately the same time frame). Concurrent validity is essential in psychodiagnostic tests. For example, if someone scores high on a test of depression, this person should also score high on any co-occurring criterion related to depression. Sample criteria for depression could include mental health professionals' ratings, behavioral observations, or self-reported behaviors. The College Stress Scale (CSS) that we introduced in Chapter 2 should have concurrent validity with behaviors that are indicative of currently experienced stress related to being in college. The CSS should not be predicting future college stress or reflecting stress experienced in the distant past.

Similarly, our example of a test measuring elements of a job can be viewed as the test items having concurrent validity with the job tasks. In work settings, a test is often used because its scores have concurrent validity with the specific requirements of a job. Unless we're going to do extensive on-the-job training, we want to know a person's ability to do a specific job immediately. In contrast, if we're going to do extensive on-the-job training, we're more interested in the ability of test scores to predict a person's ability to perform successfully after training.

A Special Case: Portfolio Assessment

Evidence for criterion-related validity is essential when portfolio assessment is the approach to measurement. Let's say you're using a portfolio assessment to select students for a graduate program in psychology. To keep this example simple, let's focus only on three criteria: (1) ability to use APA style when writing; (2) good listening skills; and (3) academic potential.

For the first criterion (the ability to use APA style when writing), experts can evaluate an applicant's written document to determine how closely it adheres to APA style. The document becomes the test, and the experts' ratings are the criterion. Information derived from these two support *concurrent validity* for the ability of the applicant at the time of writing to use APA style.

For the second criterion, good listening skills, a behavioral observation of the applicant in a structured role-play situation could yield information about his or her current ability to use listening skills. The relationship between the applicant's behaviors and the expert's ratings of these behaviors as reflecting listening skills provides evidence for *concurrent validity*.

The third criterion, academic potential, would best be measured by an aptitude test, such as the GRE, that would predict graduate school success.

Scores on this aptitude test would need to have established evidence of *predictive validity* for success in graduate school.

Two Dimensions of Concurrent Validity—Convergent and Discriminant Validity

In each of the examples given thus far, we have been talking about how test scores and the criteria converge. Significant relationships between test scores and other measures designed to assess the same construct or behavior provide evidence of *convergent validity*. The test scores and the criterion are theoretically and empirically linked.

The relationship (or nonrelationship) between test scores and measures of a construct to which the test is *not* theoretically related also provides evidence for concurrent validity, known as *discriminant validity*. For example, scores on an entrance exam for medical school should have convergent validity with grades in medical school; however, these same scores may have a weak or no relationship with ratings of physician bedside manner. This poor relationship provides evidence of discriminant validity. In this example, bedside manner is a construct different from what is being measured by the medical school entrance exam. Convergent and discriminant validity indicate not only what a test *will* predict but also what it *will not* predict.

Evidence of Construct Validity

Construct validity, sometimes referred to as *internal structural validity*, indicates the degree to which all items on a test are interrelated and measure the theoretical trait or construct the test is designed to measure. Basically, a construct is a theoretical explanation for some behavior. Construct validity is concerned with the validation of this underlying theory.

Anxiety is a theoretical construct that we can verify only by seeing how it is manifested in current behavior. Because anxiety is theoretically one construct, a test that measures anxiety should be unidimensional. Factor analysis is a statistical procedure that tests whether all items on a test contribute to that one construct. If a test is unidimensional, we expect a one-factor structure to emerge from the factor analysis.

Many tests, however, are multidimensional, making whatever is being assessed more interesting (we think). For example, the Strong Interest Inventory (SII) measures six different occupational interests: Realistic (R), Artistic (A), Investigative (I), Social (S), Enterprising (E), and Conventional (C). The theoretical foundation for the SII is Holland's conceptualization that there are six general work environments and these environments are characterized by the six occupational interests. Considerable research on the psychometric properties of the SII has consistently provided evidence supporting its underlying theory regarding a six-factor structure. Support for a six-factor structure provides some evidence of construct validity (internal structural validity) for each factor.

Items measuring a factor such as Enterprising (E) are homogeneous and contribute only to the construct validity of that factor. There is evidence that the SII yields valid scores for adult men and women across a variety of settings. The multidimensionality of the SII makes it interesting because we can interpret scores for each of the six occupational interests and create an occupational interest profile for everyone who takes the test.

A typical profile for business major Ronald Frump might be EAS. Ronald is high on Enterprising, Artistic, and Social. He can be a "killer" business person, making those hard decisions that influence the bottom line. This reflects his strong E score. His Artistic bent shows up in his creativity and ingenuity in the business world and in his extensive art collection. Ronald's propensity to be the center of attention and to be surrounded by fawning employees is a manifestation of the Social component of his occupational interests. Because there is strong evidence that the scores on the SII are valid, we can draw conclusions about Ronald and how he will manifest his occupational profile in the business world. (Watch out competitors!) If his behaviors match his profile, this lends further support for the construct validity of the SII.

Let's Check Your Understanding

We just fed you a three-course dinner. Let's see if you've started to digest each of these courses. Let's check your understanding just in case you need to review some aspect of validity.

1. What are the three major sources of evidence of validity?

   _____

   _____

2. For which source of validity evidence do you compare test items with a specific domain of information?

   _____

   _____

3. What are the two approaches for obtaining evidence for content validity?

   a. _____

   b. _____

4. What are the names given to the two major types of criterion-related validity?

   a. _____

   b. _____

5. Criterion-related validity is essential when the purpose of a test is

   a. _____

   b. _____

6. What is convergent validity?

   _____

   _____

7. What is discriminant validity?

   _____

   _____

8. Convergent and discriminant validity indicate not only what a test _____ but also what it _____.

9. Conceptually, construct validity is _____

   _____.

10. Construct validity is also referred to as _____.

11. When a single theoretical construct is being measured, the test should be _____.

12. When multiple theoretical constructs are being measured by the same test, the test should be _____ and have _____ for each construct or factor being assessed.

 ## Our Model Answers

1. What are the three major sources of evidence of validity?

   The three major sources of validity are content validity, criterion-related validity, and construct validity.

2. For which source of validity evidence do you compare test items with a specific domain of information?

   For content validity, you compare test items with a specific domain of information.

3. What are the two approaches for obtaining evidence for content validity?

    The two approaches for obtaining evidence for content validity are (a) an empirical analysis of how well the test items reflect the content domain and (b) expert ratings of the relationship between the test items and the content domain.

4. What are the names given to the two major types of criterion-related validity?

    The two major types of criterion-related validity are (a) concurrent validity and (b) predictive validity.

5. Criterion-related validity is essential when the purpose of a test is **(a) to estimate current behaviors or (b) to predict some future behavior.**

6. What is convergent validity?

    Evidence of convergent validity is shown when there is a significant relationship between test scores and other assessments of the same construct or behavior.

7. What is discriminant validity?

    Evidence of discriminant validity is shown when there is a nonsignificant relationship between test scores and measures of a construct to which the test is not theoretically related.

8. Convergent and discriminant validity indicate not only what a test **will predict** but also what it **will not predict.**

9. Conceptually, construct validity is **the degree to which all items of a test are interrelated to each other and measure the theoretical trait the test is designed to measure.**

10. Construct validity is also referred to as **internal structural validity.**

11. When a single theoretical construct is being measured, the test should be **unidimensional.**

12. When multiple theoretical constructs are being measured by the same test, the test should be **multidimensional and have validity evidence** for each construct or factor being assessed.

The Marriage of Reliability and Validity—Wedded Bliss

Both reliability and validity are essential characteristics of a good test. Like love and marriage, you can't have one without the other. Reliability and validity are even wed to each other mathematically. The validity coefficient (r_{xy}) for a test's scores cannot be greater than the square root of the test's reliability (r_{xx}). For r_{xy}, x stands for the test scores and y stands for scores on the criterion. The formula for the relationship between validity and reliability is

$$r_{xy} \leq \sqrt{r_{xx}}$$

If the reliability of a test is 0.64, the potential maximum value of the validity coefficient would be 0.80. Notice our use of the words "potential maximum value." Rarely does a validity coefficient exactly equal the square root of the reliability coefficient. It is almost always less than this potential maximum value.

Interpreting the Validity of Tests—Intended and Unintended Consequences

We mentioned high-stakes testing earlier. High-stakes testing is when test results are used to make critical decisions such as whether or not a student receives a high school diploma based on his or her test scores. This decision is based on social policy, although policy makers have tried to embed it in the realm of validity. For example, our student, John, takes a comprehensive achievement test during his senior year. This test assesses multiple dimensions of knowledge, and evidence has been provided to support its content and construct validities. An inappropriate use of this test would be to differentiate students into two groups: those who can graduate and those who can't. An achievement test is only designed to measure knowledge of content. Evidence of validity supports this purpose. Evidence of validity does not support the goal of social policy makers, to give diplomas only to those who score "high enough." Validity is always interpreted in light of the purpose of the test and should not be distorted for alternative purposes.

Some Final Thoughts About Validity

As noted by the *Standards for Educational and Psychological Testing* (1999), "A sound validity argument integrates various strands of evidence into a coherent account of the degree to which existing evidence and theory support the intended interpretation of test scores for specific uses" (p. 17). Two important concepts related to validity appear in this statement. First, more than one strand of evidence is needed for sound validity. In addition to what we have discussed in this chapter, another approach is called *multitrait multimethod* (MTMM). This approach addresses the need for more than one strand of evidence for sound validity. Two, the intended interpretation of test scores is based on validity evidence. The goal of testing is to provide meaningful information. This is only possible if there is evidence supporting the validity of the test scores. Without validity, test scores are meaningless! You might as well have read tea leaves.

Key Terms

- Validity
- Validation group
- Criterion
- Construct underrepresentation
- Construct-irrelevant variance
- Sources of validity evidence
  - Content
  - Criterion related
  - Predictive
  - Concurrent
  - Convergent
  - Discriminant
  - Internal structure
  - Construct

Models and Self-instructional Exercises

Our Model

Remember the *Honesty Inventory* (HI) you created in Chapter 9 to assess applicants for bank teller positions? We know the reliability coefficient was 0.76. Now let's see how valid scores for the HI are. Not only do you administer the HI to all applicants, you also give them the Perfectly Honest Scale (PHS) and a mathematical aptitude test. The test manual for the PHS reports a validity coefficient of 0.80 as evidence of criterion-related validity. The items on the PHS were evaluated by experts as to their measuring aspects of the construct *honesty*. The manual also reports that when the HI was given to incoming freshmen, 4 years later it discriminated between undergraduates who were elected as members of a national honor society and undergraduates who were kicked out of school for cheating. Based on what we've told you thus far:

1. What is the maximum potential validity value of the HI?

   _____

   _____

2. When you correlate applicants' HI scores with their PHS scores, what source of validity evidence are you assessing?

   _____

   _____

3. When you correlate applicants' HI scores with their mathematical aptitude test scores, what source of validity evidence are you assessing?

   _____

   _____

4. What source of validity evidence was established by the HI scores later discriminating between students in an honor society and students kicked out of school?

   _____

   _____

5. Based on the sources of validity evidence you have gathered, have you proven that the HI is a valid assessment instrument for potential bank tellers?

   _____

   _____

6. Based on your answers to questions 1 through 4, would you recommend the HI as a valid test of honesty and why?

   _____

   _____

   _____

   _____

7. An applicant who is not hired files a complaint about the job relatedness of the assessments used to screen applicants. How would you
address this complaint based on what you know?

_____

_____

_____

_____

 Our Model Answers

1. What is the maximum potential validity value of the HI?
   The validity cannot be greater than the square root of the
   reliability coefficient. To calculate the maximum potential validity value,
   we would use the formula

$$r_{xy} = \sqrt{r_{xx}}$$

$$r_{xy} = \sqrt{.76}$$

$$r_{xy} = .87$$

   Therefore, the maximum potential validity value is 0.87.

2. When you correlate applicants' HI scores with their PHS scores, what
   source of validity evidence are you assessing?
   When you correlate two measures administered at the same time
   and designed to assess the same theoretical construct, you are providing
   evidence for concurrent validity. In addition, you are providing evidence
   of construct validity since they are both based on the same theoretical
   construct.

3. When you correlate applicants' HI scores with their mathematical
   aptitude test scores, what source of validity evidence are you assessing?
   We would not expect honesty and mathematical aptitude to be theoretically linked. Therefore, the nonrelationship between these two tests
   would provide evidence for discriminant validity.

4. What source of validity evidence was established by the HI scores later
   discriminating between students in an honor society and students
   kicked out of school?
   Because the HI was administered at the beginning of the students'
   freshman year and whether they became members of the honor

society or were kicked out of school was assessed 4 years later, the HI was used to predict the future status of the students. This process provided evidence of predictive validity for HI scores.

5. Based on the sources of validity evidence you have gathered, have you proven that the HI is a valid assessment instrument for potential bank tellers?

   Although a variety of sources have provided evidence for validity of the HI, validity can *never* be proven.

6. Based on your answers to questions 1 through 4, would you recommend the HI as a valid test of honesty?

   Multiple sources of evidence for validity of the HI have been provided. Specifically, for the potential bank tellers, we've gathered evidence of concurrent, construct, and discriminant validity. We know that the validity coefficient could be as large as 0.87, which would be very strong. However, we need to remember that this is just a potential highest value, not the actual value of the validity coefficient. Furthermore, while the evidence provided for predictive validity is interesting, we need to remember that it was gathered on undergraduates, not on applicants for bank teller positions. All in all, however, we would probably recommend the HI as an assessment of honesty for applicants for bank teller positions.

7. An applicant who is not hired files a complaint about the job relatedness of the assessments used to screen applicants. How would you address this complaint based on what you know?

   Although honesty is a highly desirable characteristic in someone entrusted with other people's money, it is not directly related to the job. The mathematical aptitude test, however, would have job relatedness. Bank tellers need to know how to do math to be successful on the job. Perhaps this applicant was not hired because of a poor math aptitude score.

 ## Now It's Your Turn

Based on their scores from the HI and their mathematical aptitude test scores, you select the 50 applicants who are the most honest and have the highest math aptitude for further testing. You give them the multidimensional scale described in Chapter 9 to measure interpersonal relationships (IP) and fear of math (FOM). We know the internal consistency reliability coefficients were 0.84 for the IP scores and 0.75 for the FOM scores for the norm group of undergraduate business majors. For bank tellers who were hired, the 6-month test–retest reliabilities were 0.88 and 0.68 for these two subscales, respectively.

1. What is the maximum potential validity value of the IP for bank tellers?

$$r_{xy} = \sqrt{r_{xx}}$$

_____

_____

_____

2. What is the maximum potential validity value of the FOM for bank tellers?

_____

_____

_____

3. When you correlate applicants' FOM scores with their math aptitude scores, what source of validity evidence are you assessing?

_____

4. When you correlate applicants' IP scores with their mathematical aptitude test scores, what source of validity evidence are you assessing?

_____

5. What source of validity evidence was established when math aptitude scores were used to later predict FOM scores for those who were hired?

_____

6. What source of validity evidence was established when FOM scores were found *not* to be related to IP scores for the applicant pool?

_____

7. Based on your answers to the questions above, would you recommend the IP as a valid and reliable test of interpersonal relationships and why?

_____

_____

_____

_____

8. Based on your answers to the questions above, would you recommend the FOM as a valid and reliable test of interpersonal relationships and why?

_____

_____

_____

_____

 Our Model Answers

1. What is the maximum potential validity value of the IP for bank tellers?
   The validity cannot be greater than the square root of the reliability coefficient. The reliability coefficient we must use is the test-retest reliability coefficient, because this is the only reliability coefficient based just on bank tellers. To calculate the maximum potential validity value, we would use the formula

$$r_{xy} = \sqrt{r_{xx}}$$

$$r_{xy} = \sqrt{.88}$$

$$r_{xy} = .94$$

   Therefore, the maximum potential validity value of the IP for bank tellers is 0.94.

2. What is the maximum potential validity value of the FOM for bank tellers?
   Again, the reliability coefficient we must use is the test-retest reliability coefficient, because this is the only reliability coefficient based just on bank tellers. To calculate the maximum potential validity value, we would use the formula

$$r_{xy} = \sqrt{r_{xx}}$$

$$r_{xy} = \sqrt{.68}$$

$$r_{xy} = .82$$

Therefore, the maximum potential validity value of the FOM for bank tellers is 0.82.

3. When you correlate applicants' FOM scores with their math aptitude scores, what source of validity evidence are you assessing?

   When you correlate two measures administered at the same time and designed to assess the same or related theoretical constructs, you are providing evidence for concurrent validity, specifically convergent validity.

4. When you correlate applicants' IP scores with their mathematical aptitude test scores, what source of validity evidence are you assessing?

   When you correlate two measures administered at the same time and designed to assess the different or unrelated theoretical constructs, you are also providing evidence for concurrent validity, specifically discriminant validity.

5. What source of validity evidence was established when math aptitude scores were used to later predict FOM scores for those who were hired?

   When you use one set of scores to predict scores on a test measuring the same or a related construct and given at a later time, you are providing evidence for predictive validity.

6. What source of validity evidence was established when FOM scores were found *not* to be related to IP scores for the applicant pool?

   When you correlate two measures administered at the same time and designed to assess the different or unrelated theoretical constructs, you are again providing evidence for concurrent validity, specifically discriminant validity.

7. Based on your answers to the questions above, would you recommend the IP as a valid and reliable test of interpersonal relationships and why?

   Yes. Its maximum potential validity coefficient was 0.94. The IP had a test-retest reliability of 0.88 for bank tellers, and an internal consistency reliability of 0.84 for undergraduate business majors. In addition, the SE_m of 1.6 is relatively small for the applicant pool. Taken collectively, the IP appears to be a reliable and valid measure of interpersonal relationships for bank tellers.

8. Based on your answers to the questions above, would you recommend the FOM as a valid and reliable test of interpersonal relationships and why?

> Maybe. Its maximum potential validity coefficient was 0.82. The FOM had a test-retest reliability of only 0.68 for bank tellers, and an internal consistency reliability of 0.75 for undergraduate business majors. These are weak reliability coefficients. However, the SE_m of 1.1 is relatively small for the applicant pool. Taken collectively, the FOM is not a particularly reliable measure of fear of math for bank tellers, even though the maximum potential validity coefficient is 0.82. This would be a good time to emphasize that this value is only a "maximum potential." The actual validity could be much lower.

 # Words of Encouragement

Hurray, hurray, hurray! You have mastered all the basic technical aspects of measurement and testing that we have covered in this user-friendly guide. We hope we have piqued your interest in measurement. If we have, and you are thinking about pursuing more course work in tests and measurement and then applying this information in a job setting, our last chapter on the perils and pitfalls of testing will be of particular interest to you.

CHAPTER 11

The Perils and Pitfalls of Testing—Being Ethical

L et's pretend that you are passing this class with flying colors—red, white, and blue, of course—and are thinking about actually using your newfound knowledge of measurement and testing. This means that you need to pay particularly close attention to this last chapter—The Perils and Pitfalls of Testing.

There are two large ethical domains that you ethically need to be concerned about. These are your own competence and the rights of the people you test or assess.

Your Own Competence

If you want our honest appraisal of your competence at this point in time, we would have to tell you that you are *not* ready to administer and interpret tests. What you probably are prepared to do is

1. Read test manuals critically to determine whether a test is appropriate for a given purpose, whether it is reliable and valid, and whether there are appropriate norm groups.

2. Understand and interpret a test score in the abstract without using it to make decisions about someone's life.

We know that this doesn't seem like much, but remember that the primary reason for testing is to help someone make very personal decisions. The person being tested usually has a lot at risk, so we want to make sure that whoever administers and interprets his or her test is really skilled and knowledgeable. You've just begun learning about measurement issues. There are a ton of things you don't know. You need to take advanced measurement courses and courses in applying your knowledge with specific tests before you even consider doing testing.

Another potential use of the knowledge we have tried to impart in this book is helping with test construction. If you were to get a position in a testing company such as Psychological Corporation and if you worked with a team, you might just be a very good choice to help develop and standardize psychological instruments. You know what has to be done even if you don't know how to do it yourself.

Primarily, however, we believe that you are almost ready to be a critical consumer of measurement issues and test results. For example, if you are a teacher, we hope we have instilled in you a reasonable caution about interpreting test scores and about using single test scores to make any educational decisions, as well as a concern about item difficulty and discrimination. If you are in business and industry, we hope you think carefully before using test scores for hiring or promotion decisions and are careful to ensure that any test used has "job relatedness." Most of all, we hope you respect the rights of those who have been tested.

Rights of Those Being Tested

Let's say you have continued your education and are truly ready to administer and interpret tests. Again, you have many ethical responsibilities. Just a few of these are

1. You must ensure that the test you have chosen has strong psychometric qualities—reliability and validity.

2. If you are using a norm-referenced test, you need to make sure that the norm group is appropriate for the person you are going to test.

3. You need to protect the confidentiality of the person you are testing.

4. You need to protect the test itself, answer sheets, and responses from being shared with someone who is not competent in testing.

5. You need to make sure that you do not "overinterpret" test scores.

6. You need to be careful not to use test scores in a way that is harmful.

We know that we have placed a lot of "you must" and "you need to" in this list. But becoming involved in measurement issues is a serious undertaking. The results reflect on people and how they are viewed. This is a heavy responsibility for anyone who develops a test, who selects a test, who administers a test, and who interprets test results. Not only are they held responsible for the confidentiality of anyone who takes a test, they are also responsible for keeping confident all aspects of the test itself. Tests are to be used only by those who are competent and this includes having access to actual tests.

Points 5 and 6 are particularly important to us as psychologists. Do you remember our friend Ryan in the beginning chapters? He took both a college stress test and a social support test at the college counseling center. What if his stress level had been so high that he was suicidal? What if his social support system was totally nonexistent and he was on the verge of quitting school? When the counselor chose to test him, the counselor assumed the responsibility of using the results to help Ryan. To accomplish this, the counselor had to be conscious of the potential dangers of testing and of the responsibility to protect Ryan's rights.

Potential Dangers

Three major dangers of testing have been frequently written about in the literature. The first is "invasion of privacy." When you ask someone to answer any test or measurement questions, you are asking about personal thoughts, ideas, knowledge, or attitudes. By answering the questions, they are revealing personal information about themselves. We have an ethical obligation to respect this information and to keep it confidential.

The second major danger of testing is "self-incrimination." Sometimes our test or measurement questions ask about information that most people would not talk about. For example, if someone takes a personality inventory, questions about certain behaviors are asked. Remember our Honesty Inventory? If our job applicants answered the items honestly, they may well have been giving us "involuntary confessions" of behaviors that may be illegal. Based on their answers, not only did they get or not get hired, they also got a label—honest or not honest. Before a person ever answers test questions, they need to know who will see their test scores and what will happen to them as a result of their responses.

The last major danger of testing is "unfair discrimination." We want tests and all measurement devices to be reliable and valid and to help us discriminate among individuals, not against people. For example, the profiles Gandalf obtained for Mr. Frodo and Samwise Gamgee helped him make a decision about who would be the ring bearer. Test results can help us decide who will be the best for certain tasks or jobs, who has mastered specific bodies of knowledge, who needs further assistance or help in an area, or who has a special aptitude. What we don't want a test to do is to discriminate against a person or group of people. When a test is not culturally sensitive or when it is given in a language that someone has not mastered, it will discriminate against that person. Remember, it is unethical to use test results to discriminate against a group of people. So, if your test promotes Euro-American children and puts other children (Native Americans, Latinos, or African Americans) into special education classes, it is unfairly discriminating against these children of color and is culturally biased. America has a sad history of using tests to "categorize and separate" that we are trying to overcome. Be one of the good guys; use your knowledge of measurement to help others, not to hurt them.

Ryan's Rights

Embedded in the dangers are the rights of clients or students or potential employees. We need to protect their right to privacy, to know when their answers might be self-incriminating, and to trust that test scores will not be used to discriminate against them in any way. Specifically, Ryan has the right to know his test scores will not be shared with his professors, classmates, or anyone else without his consent. He has the right to know that some test items might ask about incriminating behaviors. This implies that he also has the right to refuse to answer these questions. Finally, he has the right to know that his test scores will not be used against him. That is, he has the right to know how the test scores will be used and to have veto power over any projected use.

Whenever you are involved in testing people, they have the right to give "informed consent" before they are tested. This consent should (1) tell them about the test, what use will be made of the results, who will see the results, and perhaps even how long the test results will be kept; (2) be given freely or voluntarily by the person who will be tested; and (3) be given only by a person who is competent to understand what he or she is consenting to. If the person being tested is a minor, consent must be obtained from a parent or guardian. In addition, the minor should be asked to give informed assent; that is, they agree to be tested and know what is being asked of them.

Often schools administer tests to every student. When this happens, they are acting "in loco parentis." If testing is mandated by the state, the school does not need to obtain specific consent from the parents. However, if a school system agrees to let you test students for your personal research, you must get affirmative parental consent. We use the term *affirmative* to indicate that you must have signed consent. Failure to say no is not consent!

As you evolve in your knowledge of measurement and testing, we just want to remind you to be ethical and to respect the power of tests. We believe in you!! In fact, we believe in you so much, there is no "Let's Check Your Understanding" for this chapter.

Appendix

Areas Beneath the Normal Curve

Z Score	Area Between the Mean and the Z Score	Z Score	Area Between the Mean and the Z Score	Z Score	Area Between the Mean and the Z Score	Z Score	Area Between the Mean and the Z Score	Z Score	Area Between the Mean and the Z Score	Z Score	Area Between the Mean and the Z Score	Z Score	Area Between the Mean and the Z Score	Z Score	Area Between the Mean and the Z Score
0.00	0.00	0.50	19.15	1.00	34.13	1.50	43.32	2.00	47.72	2.50	49.38	3.00	49.87	3.50	49.98
0.01	0.40	0.52	19.50	1.01	34.38	1.51	43.45	2.01	47.78	2.51	49.40	3.01	49.87	3.51	49.98
0.02	0.50	0.53	19.85	1.02	34.61	1.52	43.57	2.02	47.83	2.52	49.41	3.02	49.87	3.52	49.98
0.03	1.20	0.54	20.19	1.03	34.85	1.53	43.70	2.03	47.88	2.53	49.43	3.03	49.88	3.53	49.98
0.04	1.60	0.55	20.54	1.04	35.08	1.54	43.82	2.04	47.93	2.54	49.45	3.04	49.88	3.54	49.98
0.05	1.99	0.56	20.88	1.05	35.31	1.55	43.94	2.05	47.98	2.55	49.46	3.05	49.89	3.55	49.98
0.06	2.39	0.57	21.23	1.06	35.54	1.56	44.06	2.06	48.03	2.56	49.48	3.06	49.89	3.56	49.98
0.07	2.79	0.58	21.57	1.07	35.77	1.57	44.18	2.07	48.08	2.57	49.49	3.07	49.89	3.57	49.98
0.08	3.19	0.59	21.90	1.08	35.99	1.58	44.29	2.08	48.12	2.58	49.51	3.08	49.9	3.58	49.98
0.09	3.59	0.60	22.24	1.09	36.21	1.59	44.41	2.09	48.17	2.59	49.52	3.09	49.9	3.59	49.98
0.10	3.98	0.61	22.57	1.10	36.43	1.60	44.52	2.10	48.21	2.60	49.53	3.10	49.9	3.60	49.98
0.11	4.38	0.62	22.91	1.11	36.65	1.61	44.63	2.11	48.26	2.61	49.55	3.11	49.91	3.61	49.98
0.12	4.78	0.63	23.24	1.12	36.86	1.62	44.74	2.12	48.30	2.62	49.56	3.12	49.91	3.62	49.98
0.13	5.17	0.64	23.57	1.13	37.08	1.63	44.84	2.13	48.34	2.63	49.57	3.13	49.91	3.63	49.98
0.14	5.57	0.65	23.89	1.14	37.29	1.64	44.95	2.14	48.38	2.64	49.59	3.14	49.92	3.64	49.98
0.15	5.96	0.66	24.54	1.15	37.49	1.65	45.05	2.15	48.42	2.65	49.60	3.15	49.92	3.65	49.98
0.16	6.36	0.67	24.86	1.16	37.70	1.66	45.15	2.16	48.46	2.66	49.61	3.16	49.92	3.66	49.98
0.17	6.75	0.68	25.17	1.17	37.90	1.67	45.25	2.17	48.50	2.67	49.62	3.17	49.92	3.67	49.98
0.18	7.14	0.69	25.49	1.18	38.10	1.68	45.35	2.18	48.54	2.68	49.63	3.18	49.93	3.68	49.98
0.19	7.53	0.70	25.80	1.19	38.30	1.69	45.45	2.19	48.57	2.69	49.64	3.19	49.93	3.69	49.98
0.20	7.93	0.71	26.11	1.20	38.49	1.70	45.54	2.20	48.61	2.70	49.65	3.20	49.93	3.70	49.99

Areas Beneath the Normal Curve

Z Score	Area Between the Mean and the Z Score	Z Score	Area Between the Mean and the Z Score	Z Score	Area Between the Mean and the Z Score	Z Score	Area Between the Mean and the Z Score	Z Score	Area Between the Mean and the Z Score	Z Score	Area Between the Mean and the Z Score	Z Score	Area Between the Mean and the Z Score	Z Score	Area Between the Mean and the Z Score
0.21	8.32	0.72	26.42	1.21	38.69	1.71	45.64	2.21	48.64	2.71	49.66	3.21	49.93	3.71	49.99
0.22	8.71	0.73	26.73	1.22	38.88	1.72	45.73	2.22	48.68	2.72	49.67	3.22	49.94	3.72	49.99
0.23	9.10	0.74	27.04	1.23	39.07	1.73	45.82	2.23	48.71	2.73	49.68	3.23	49.94	3.73	49.99
0.24	9.48	0.75	27.34	1.24	39.25	1.74	45.91	2.24	48.75	2.74	49.69	3.24	49.94	3.74	49.99
0.25	0.99	0.76	27.64	1.25	39.44	1.75	45.99	2.25	45.78	2.75	49.70	3.25	49.94	3.75	49.99
0.26	10.26	0.77	27.94	1.26	39.62	1.76	46.08	2.26	48.81	2.76	49.71	3.26	49.94	3.76	49.99
0.27	10.64	0.78	28.23	1.27	39.80	1.77	46.16	2.27	48.84	2.77	49.72	3.27	49.94	3.77	49.99
0.28	11.03	0.79	28.52	1.28	39.97	1.78	46.25	2.28	48.87	2.78	49.73	3.28	49.94	3.78	49.99
0.29	11.41	0.80	28.81	1.29	40.15	1.79	46.33	2.29	48.90	2.79	49.74	3.29	49.94	3.79	49.99
0.30	11.79	0.81	29.10	1.30	40.32	1.80	46.41	2.30	48.93	2.80	49.74	3.30	49.95	3.80	49.99
0.31	12.17	0.82	29.39	1.31	40.49	1.81	46.49	2.31	48.96	2.81	49.75	3.31	49.95	3.81	49.99
0.32	12.55	0.83	29.67	1.32	40.66	1.82	46.56	2.32	48.98	2.82	49.76	3.32	49.95	3.82	49.99
0.33	12.93	0.84	29.95	1.33	40.82	1.83	46.64	2.33	49.01	2.83	49.77	3.33	49.95	3.83	49.99
0.34	13.31	0.85	30.23	1.34	40.99	1.84	46.71	2.34	49.04	2.84	49.77	3.34	49.95	3.84	49.99
0.35	13.68	0.86	30.51	1.35	41.15	1.85	46.78	2.35	49.06	2.85	49.78	3.35	49.96	3.85	49.99
0.36	14.06	0.87	30.78	1.36	41.31	1.86	46.86	2.36	49.09	2.86	49.79	3.36	49.96	3.86	49.99
0.37	14.43	0.88	31.06	1.37	41.47	1.87	46.93	2.37	49.11	2.87	49.79	3.37	49.96	3.87	49.99
0.38	14.80	0.89	31.33	1.38	41.62	1.88	46.99	2.38	49.13	2.88	49.80	3.38	49.96	3.88	49.99
0.39	15.17	0.90	31.59	1.39	41.77	1.89	47.06	2.39	49.16	2.89	49.81	3.39	49.96	3.89	49.99
0.40	15.54	0.91	31.86	1.40	41.92	1.90	47.13	2.40	49.18	2.90	49.81	3.40	49.97	3.90	49.99

(Continued)

Areas Beneath the Normal Curve (Continued)

Z Score	Area Between the Mean and the Z Score	Z Score	Area Between the Mean and the Z Score	Z Score	Area Between the Mean and the Z Score	Z Score	Area Between the Mean and the Z Score	Z Score	Area Between the Mean and the Z Score	Z Score	Area Between the Mean and the Z Score
0.41	15.91	0.92	32.12	1.41	42.07	1.91	47.19	2.41	49.20	2.91	49.82	3.41	49.97	3.91	49.99
0.42	16.28	0.93	32.38	1.42	42.22	1.92	47.26	2.42	49.22	2.92	49.82	3.42	49.97	3.92	49.99
0.43	16.64	0.94	32.64	1.43	42.36	1.93	47.32	2.43	49.25	2.93	49.83	3.43	49.97	3.93	49.99
0.44	17.00	0.95	32.89	1.44	42.51	1.94	47.38	2.44	49.27	2.94	49.84	3.44	49.97	3.94	49.99
0.45	17.36	0.96	33.15	1.45	42.65	1.95	47.44	2.45	49.29	2.95	49.84	3.45	49.98	3.95	49.99
0.46	17.72	0.97	33.40	1.46	42.79	1.96	47.50	2.46	49.31	2.96	49.85	3.46	49.98	3.96	49.99
0.47	18.08	0.98	33.65	1.47	42.92	1.97	47.56	2.47	49.32	2.97	49.85	3.47	49.98	3.97	49.99
0.48	18.44	0.99	33.89	1.48	43.06	1.98	47.61	2.48	49.34	2.98	49.86	3.48	49.98	3.98	49.99
0.49	18.79	1.00	34.13	1.49	43.19	1.99	47.67	2.49	49.36	2.99	49.86	3.49	49.98	3.99	49.99

References

Anastasi, A., & Urbina, S. (1997). *Psychological testing.* Upper Saddle River, NJ: Prentice-Hall.

Dick, W., & Hagerty, N. (1971). *Topics in measurement: Reliability and validity.* New York: McGraw-Hill.

Gloria, A. M., & Robinson Kurpius, S. E. (1996). African American students' persistence at a predominantly white university: Influences of social support, university comfort, and self-beliefs. *Journal of College Student Development, 40,* 257–268.

Kranzler, G., & Moursund, J. (1999). *Statistics for the terrified* (2nd ed.). Upper Saddle River, NJ: Prentice-Hall.

Robinson, S. E. (1992). *The adolescent at-risk behaviors inventory.* Unpublished test. Tempe, AZ: Arizona State University.

Rosenberg, M. S. (1979). *Conceiving the self.* New York: Basic Books.

Salkind, N. J. (2004). *Statistics for people who think they hate statistics* (2nd ed.). Thousand Oaks, CA: Sage.

Standards for educational and psychological testing (1999). Washington, D.C.: American Educational Research Association, American Psychological Association, and National Council on Measurement in Education.

Stevens, S. S. (1946). On the theory of scales of measurement. *Science, 103,* 677–680.

Index

Absolute zero, 4, 5
Adolescent At-Risk Behaviors
    Inventory, 14–18
Alternate forms reliability, 126–127
Analysis, item, 112
Anastasi, A., 115
Anchors, 8
Average:
    calculation of mean, 53–54
    standard deviation and, 60, 61

Behavioral sciences, 5
Bell-shaped curve.
    See Normal curve
Bimodal curve, 48, 49
Binet IV, 85
Biserial correlation, 117

California Personality Inventory, 84
CCS (Cultural Congruity Scale), 111
Central tendencies:
    cartoon of, 48
    choice of measurement, 57
    definition of, 47
    key terms, 63
    mean, 53–54
    median, 50–52
    medians, modes, for grouped
        frequency data, 53
    mode, 48–49
    models/exercises for, 64–70
    questions/answers about,
        49–50, 52–53, 54–56

cf. See Cumulative frequency
Class interval:
    in cumulative frequency
        distribution, 26–27
    in grouped frequency distribution,
        22–24
    mode and, 49
    of grouped frequency data, 53
Class interval width, 22, 73–74
Cohen's Kappa, 130
College Stress Scale (CSS):
    concurrent validity for, 149
    in frequency curve model,
        42–43
    in frequency distribution model,
        28–31
    mode of scores, 49–50
    response formats and, 7–8, 11
    Z scores and, 80, 81–83
Competence, tester, 163–164
Concurrent validity, 149, 150
Confidence interval, 132–133
Confidentiality, testee, 164
Consent, informed, 166
Consistency, 121
Construct
    underrepresentation, 145
Construct validity, 150–151
Construct-irrelevant variance:
    description of, 145
    test content and, 147–148
Content stability, 127–129
Content validity, 147–148

About the Authors

Sharon E. Robinson Kurpius, Ph.D., received her doctoral degree from Indiana University. She double majored in Counseling Psychology and Educational Inquiry Methodology. Upon graduation, she left the wintry Midwest to join the counseling faculty at Arizona State University. As a professor at ASU, she has taught a variety of courses such as Research and Evaluation, Research in Counseling, Psychological Testing, Professional Ethics, Health and Wellness, and Doctoral Practicum. She has received many national grants to study alcohol and substance abuse among adolescents, to work with talented at-risk teenage girls, to teach college professors and high school teachers how to be more effective in keeping girls and minorities in math and the sciences, and to bring engineering concepts to the K–12 classroom. In addition to her work as a professor, she is actively involved in psychological consultation and has worked with major telephone companies, hospitals, and mental health agencies to improve quality of work life. Of the things she likes to do best, the most liked is playing with her granddaughter, followed by riding horses in the Colorado mountains, skiing blue and green slopes in Utah, or reading a good book.

Mary E. Stafford, Ph.D., has been a faculty member in the School Psychology Program in the Division of Psychology in Education at Arizona State University and is a faculty member in the School Psychology Program at the University of Houston Clear Lake. She teaches courses in child counseling, diagnosis and interventions with emotionally handicapped children and adolescents, physiological bases of behavior, statistics, applied research in school psychology, and intellectual assessment. Previously, she has worked with children in public school and residential treatment center settings as a math teacher, counselor, psychometrician, and school principal. She received her Ph.D. in educational psychology with an emphasis in school psychology from the University of Texas at Austin. Her research and writing have focused on psychometric issues of personality and vocational tests, at-risk children's achievement and adjustment in schools, resiliency, and socioeconomic and cultural issues in mental health. Her hobbies include hiking in the mountains, going to the symphony, and reading.